YOU
Let's Cook 4

TESTED BY
YOU

YOU
Let's Cook **4**

Carmen Niehaus

Human & Rousseau
Cape Town Pretoria Johannesburg

This book was not written in isolation. Many people contributed; from those hospitable people all over the country who opened their homes to us and so generously shared their recipes, to photographers, copy editors and layout artists. A sincere thank you to the photographers, David Briers, Adriaan Oosthuizen and Neville Lockhart, who accompanied me on my travels across the country, were prepared to sacrifice their weekends and to sleep in unfamiliar beds. In addition, I wish to thank Wilma Howells, creative director of *You*, who styled a few of the food photographs and who helped with the final selection of photographs; and Arina du Plessis who saw to it that all the recipes were thoroughly tested.

Thank you also to Magda Herbst for the typing of the recipes, Anelma Ruschioni and Lesley Krige for coordinating the publication, Annelene van der Merwe for translation from the Afrikaans, Pat Barton for copy-editing, and Etienne van Duyker for the book's layout.

Photo acknowledgments:

David Briers:
pp. 12 (bottom one), 18, 20, 21, 28, 32 (centre), 36, 43, 45, 46, 47, 48, 69, 70,
71, 104, 106, 107, 108, 109, 110, 111, 112, 113, 114, 120, 121, 122, 123, 148 (bottom two),
156, 158, 159, 160, 162, 163, 164, 165, 166, 167, 168, 169, 170, 171, 172, 173, 174, 184, 188,
191, 192, 194, 196, 197, 199, 200, 201, 203, 204, 206, 207, 209, 211, 212, 214, 215, 216

Adriaan Oosthuizen:
pp. 10, 12 (centre two), 22, 23, 24, 25, 27, 30, 31, 32 (top and bottom), 33, 35, 37, 39, 40, 41, 42,
52 (centre and bottom), 53, 54, 56, 57, 63 (bottom), 68, 73, 74, 76, 77, 79, 80, 81, 83, 84, 86, 88, 89,
90, 91, 93, 95, 97, 98, 101, 102, 106 (second from top), 115, 116, 118, 119, 124, 126, 127, 128, 129,
130, 131, 132, 133, 134, 136, 137, 138, 139, 140, 141, 142, 143, 144, 146, 148 (top two), 149, 151,
152, 153, 176, 177, 178, 179, 180, 182, 186, 187

Neville Lockhart:
pp. 11 (small photo), 12 (top three), 13, 14, 15, 17, 50, 52 (top), 58, 59, 60, 61, 62, 63 (top), 64, 66,
82, 218, 220, 221, 222, 223, 224, 225, 229, 231, 232, 234, 235, 236, 237

Copyright © 2001 strictly reserved
First published in 2001 by Human & Rousseau (Pty) Ltd,
28 Wale Street, Cape Town
Styling by Carmen Niehaus
Typography and cover design by Etienne van Duyker
Text electronically prepared and typeset in 10 on 12 pt Avante Garde by ALINEA STUDIO, Cape Town
Printed and bound by NBD, Drukkery Street, Cape Town, South Africa

ISBN 0 7981 4073 9

Contents

In search

This book has a special significance for me because, while I was putting it together, the photographs and recipes brought back wonderful memories of all the unforgettable experiences that came my way during the ten years or so that I travelled the country in search of good food. But let me add, right from the start, that for this book we didn't even come close to visiting all the beautiful parts of the country or meeting all the expert cooks out there – there simply wasn't enough time. But the warmth and generosity showered on me at the places I did reach have convinced me that South Africans are truly hospitable, whether they live a stone's throw from Table Mountain or in the farflung corners of the Kalahari. And of their superior cooking abilities there can be no doubt whatsoever.

The flavour of food, its taste and smell have always inspired me – after all, it's the taste of delicious food that we remember. Today's hurried lifestyle seems to have robbed us of the ability to use our senses to the full – we look but don't see, hear but don't listen, touch but don't feel, chew but don't taste. We've forgotten how things taste and, at the same time, the memories they awoke in us. If we think back to our childhood, we often find that it's a special food our mothers used to make that we long for; that special dish no one else can make in just the same way. And then we cherish that memory in our hearts, almost afraid to share it with anyone else.

In 2000, at the first Windhoek arts festival, I spent some delightful hours with a group of *You* readers. At the Craft Centre we chatted at length about all the good memories tasty food awakens in us. I'd brought along a tin of spices for each of them; as we dug out one spice after the other from the tins I started thinking back, and later we all happily shared our recollections.

During my visit to Windhoek I explored the city thoroughly. Elsabé Retief, our hostess, showed us all the best eating places, but the outing I remember best was the picnic, with *Brötchens* and smoked meats, under the camel-thorn tree close to Windhoek cemetery. I also remember, later that weekend, on Joof and

# of good food

Marina Lampbrecht's safari farm, the glasses of sweet sherry that warmed us after we returned from a game-viewing drive, drenched to the skin.

Our first stop in Namibia was in the south, at Noachabeb, which nestles among the hills of the Karasberg. Here, in the middle of the sand flats, we laid a table with damask and crystal, silver and the family crockery. The food was a feast of game dishes accompanied by roast potatoes and pumpkin fritters. Long after the sun had disappeared behind the mountain, we were still savouring these special moments while we emptied our glasses to the last drop.

I can never get enough of the wilderness – and what an experience it was to view game from the air! It was bitterly cold when Chris Alberts and Sampie Ras once again took us up in their microlites. Later we landed in a clearing in the middle of the bush. A steaming mug of coffee – I think it was black, otherwise you'd have to add Cremora – tasted heavenly with what were definitely the most delicious rusks I'd ever had; I remember they had an aniseed flavour.

The Kalahari with its rust-brown sand dunes has an allure all its own. On Kiepietjiegorra, the farm belonging to the parents of my former assistant, Lizbé Jonas, the staple food is game biltong. It's always plentiful, and each piece is generously sprinkled with toasted coriander. While we were the guests of Duineveld High School we rode on camels and slid down sand dunes, and picnicked on griddlecakes and milk tartlets on the edge of a vast salt pan, deep in the heart of the Kalahari. But Le Must in Upington stands out; I simply couldn't get enough of their sumptuous food – from braised tomatoes with potato cakes and roasted vegetables to pumpkin risotto and biltong soup, not to mention the spring onions, deep-fried and sprinkled with balsamic vinegar.

My colleagues and I have spent many a fun-filled hour on the beach at Saldanha. We spent a weekend in a charmingly dilapidated stone cottage perched on a dune, dreaming up some exciting new ideas for the food pages. We ate paella and braaied sosaties; we baked small loaves of bread in tins and nibbled white lamingtons while having fun on the beach.

We also like to do things in style sometimes. At Blue Bay Lodge, also in Saldanha, we dined at wooden tables from Bali, and Mariaan Wicht served her food with flair. The dinner menu consisted of roast leg of lamb with an unusual yoghurt sauce, partnered by delectable oven-baked vegetables sprinkled with mustard and cumin seeds. I discovered, at the same time, that Mariaan and I had been at university together and had done the same course.

Liz Southey, who occasionally helped me with styling in *You*'s kitchen, also has a Karoo farm, in the Colesberg district. At her invitation we spent a week in this pretty Karoo town. I soon discovered that, contrary to what people might think, this was not just a town to pass through on your way to somewhere else. Apart from the delectable soup and peri-peri chicken livers we enjoyed at the pub in town, it was the *Lady Laatvy* trip on the Orange River I will never forget – perhaps because of the moon shining through the clouds on the return trip. Or perhaps it was the incredible flavour rosemary lent to the leg of venison braaied over the coals that stuck in my memory; served with griddlecakes, this will remain food fit for a king. I even sampled pan-fried barbel and nibbled peri-peri biltong – you'd never say it was made from goat's meat.

In Graaff-Reinet I learnt a few cooking secrets from Beatrice Barnard of the Andries Stockenström guesthouse. Wearing her chef's jacket, she prepared French-style dinners every night. The flavour combinations were unsurpassable, and I discovered anew how important it is to keep on tasting until the flavour is just right. Skimping was not tolerated here. Everything was absolutely fresh: the salad greens came from the garden and the fruit and nuts were harvested from trees in the back yard. Long after the other guests had gone to bed, we sat chatting at the kitchen table, sharing cookery secrets: an inspiration to any aspiring cook.

Another person for whom cooking is a passion is Laetitia Prinsloo of The Institute of Culinary Arts on the Spier estate outside Stellenbosch. Not only does she believe that the youth of this country has extraordinary drive; she's also convinced that we're finally establishing our own food culture and that it will eventually enjoy international recognition.

I love paging through cookery books, and Leipoldt's have been a source of

great inspiration over the years. He's so charmingly casual about food that it makes you want to try the recipes – and besides, they're written so beautifully. So I think it's a great idea that the people of Clanwilliam, Leipoldt's birthplace, again hold a Leipoldt festival, where they cook dishes from his books – with ginger and aniseed, naartjie peel and cinnamon, those wonderful flavours he loved so much. It rained on the day of our visit, and I remember the delightful aromas wafting up our nostrils as we laid a table set up on the pavement, and trying to cope with the showers and umbrellas at the same time.

Today, the foods from our past are being served with renewed enthusiasm. And where better than at the Castle, where our unique cuisine was born? In 2000 one of my assistants, Wilma Howells, got married there, and we did a beautiful, suitably nostalgic feature about a Castle wedding. The dishes were a model of new-style boerekos, flavoursome and attractively presented: bobotie with a delicious Malay flavour acquired a spring roll jacket; there were sweet potatoes and pumpkin fritters and, for dessert, small pavlovas with prickly pear cream – all truly South African.

I've attended many festivals, but these days Oudtshoorn is the cherry on top. I don't think for a moment that anyone thought an Afrikaans festival could become so big. The festival-goers also had to eat, so eateries and kiosks sprang up on the streets, literally overnight. Food was to be had everywhere, with braaied meat and griddlecakes naturally the most popular. Oudtshoorn's established restaurants earned my undying respect, however: they had to feed the multitudes from morning to night and managed always to serve good food. The Le Roux sisters' restaurant, Jemima's, was the talk of the town and you could find all the well-known personalities there. Naturally, their festive table groaned under a wealth of delectable dishes. The food was simple, but still a combination of old and new, served with style. It was well prepared, without skimping or taking short cuts, and combined the most delicious flavours that complemented one another perfectly. I also know where Annette learnt to cook – on the old Aga stove in her mother's kitchen at Domein Doornkraal, where Ann le Roux serves the most irresistible dishes. Believe me, I know – I've also been there.

Cape of **plenty**

Table Mountain has been standing guard over the waters of Table Bay for untold centuries. And at its foot lies the Mother City, with its interesting mixture of cultures and its rich heritage from an eventful past.

The city moves at a leisurely pace, inviting you to relax and see all its wonderful sights. At the waterfront lie yachts, tightly packed at the quay; eateries in well-known streets beckon you, offering anything from coffee and cake to outstanding dishes from foreign shores. On the outskirts of the city you will still find working farms complete with a farmstall in a barn, where chickens nest among the herbs and buchu and guests sit down to cheeses arranged on tin plates and served with lemon syrup or coffee.

The cuisine ranges from cosmopolitan to modern South African, but here and there are dishes Jan van Riebeeck would also have enjoyed.

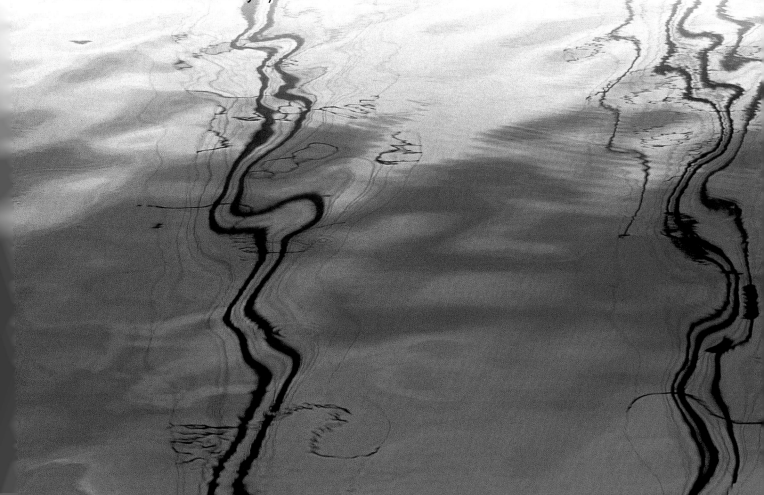

The Castle is undoubtedly a well-known landmark in the city. Long ago it was the cultural centre of the city, and it is finally beginning to regain its former glory. You can now get married there or hold other functions, and ride in an old cart or coach; there are guards along the cobbled road and a piper or a military band supplies the music.

In Tokai, on the way to Pollsmoor prison, an old barn was rebuilt and converted into a unique farm shop. All the products are home-made – you'll search in vain for a packet of cigarettes or Simba chips among the salad dressings, herb vinegars, jams, olives, pickles, chutney, pasta and eggs laid by the farm's own chickens. Even the soaps, reed brooms and fly swatters are home-made. You can still select your dried fruit and sun-dried tomatoes from large baskets and pack them yourself in brown paperbags, take a hot loaf from the shelf and wait while honey is tapped for you.

Just before the New Year of '99, I was inspired once more by the enthusiasm and positive attitude of others. Heidi Vollmer of Heidi's Coffee Shop in Cavendish Square, Claremont, never lets herself be defeated, not even by a physical handicap. Heidi and her husband, Russel, are great yachting enthusiasts and, at her suggestion, we did the photo session on a yacht in Cape Town harbour. With a tray balanced on her lap, Heidi filled platters with eats for a festive New Year's party. At dusk we drank a toast to an enjoyable day of working together, and I couldn't but admire this courageous woman who, despite her handicap, embraces every day and enjoys it to the full.

The Castle is again becoming the cultural centre it once was. A blacksmith and a Castle shop have reappeared, and a bakery is planned. Then, of course, there is the restaurant appropriately named De Goewerneur. From the outset, Harrie Siertsema and Herman Kotze wanted to treat their guests to familiar foods. Harrie has given traditional South African dishes a new twist, adding a touch of Malay flavour and serving them in original ways; bobotie, for example, is served in a spring roll jacket or baked in individual portions; chicken pie is also served in individual dishes. The sweet potatoes are, without doubt, the most delectable in the country – the recipe is his mother's, and so are the recipes for the brandy tart and milk tart.

Harrie also serves foods remembered from his youth: malva pudding and bread and butter pudding, Malay curries and bredies (stews). The menus often have a theme – for example, Cape Malay, and then they invite the Cape Minstrels or Malay choirs to perform for their guests.

Bobotie spring rolls

25 g butter

30 ml (2 T) olive oil

15 ml (1 T) grated fresh ginger

15 ml (1 T) brown sugar

7 ml (1½ t) curry powder

7 ml (1½ t) turmeric

5 ml (1 t) salt

2 chives, finely chopped

500 g mince

1 slice white bread, crusts removed
   and soaked in

125 ml (½ c) milk

75 ml (5 T) raisins, soaked in port

25 ml (5 t) chutney

10 ml (2 t) apricot jam

10 ml (2 t) vinegar

10 ml (2 t) Worcester sauce

15 ml (1 T) tomato sauce

75 ml (5 T) finely sliced dried apricots

100 ml almond slivers, toasted

1 packet (500 g) phyllo pastry

melted butter

oil for deep-frying

Melt the butter and olive oil in a heavy-based saucepan and add the ginger, brown sugar, curry powder, turmeric, salt and chives. Stir-fry until the chives are tender. Add the mince and brown slightly. Mash the white bread with a fork and add to the mince, along with the raisins, chutney, apricot jam, vinegar, Worcester sauce, tomato sauce, apricots and almonds. Simmer for 10-15 minutes and cool.

Cut two layers of phyllo pastry into six uniform squares. Top each square with a little of the mince mixture, fold in the sides and roll up. Brush the loose ends with melted butter, fold over and secure to the roll. Heat the oil and fry the rolls until golden brown. Drain and serve hot.

Makes 10-12 rolls.

*A selecton of snacks with
(front right) bobotie spring rolls*

Warm ostrich fillet salad with berry dressing

100 g mixed salad leaves

1 packet mangetout

1 tin (410 g) mixed berries, drained

250 ml (1 c) red wine vinegar

30 ml (2 T) castor sugar

140 g ostrich fillet, sliced into strips

olive oil

butter

salt and freshly ground black pepper to taste

Arrange the salad leaves and mangetout on each plate. Place the berries, vinegar and castor sugar in a saucepan and heat until the sugar has dissolved. Bring to the boil and simmer for 1-2 minutes.

Fry the ostrich strips in the olive oil and butter until just done. Season with salt and pepper and arrange on top of the salad leaves. Drizzle the hot dressing over the salad and season to taste with salt and freshly ground black pepper.

Serves 4.

Glazed sweet potatoes

1,5 kg sweet potatoes, peeled and sliced

100 ml butter

20 ml (4 t) water

3 pieces dried naartjie peel

2 pieces stick cinnamon, crushed

5 ml (1 t) salt

250 ml (1 c) yellow sugar

30 ml (2 T) honey

Place all the ingredients in a heavy-based saucepan. Heat over medium heat until all the water has evaporated. Shake the saucepan occasionally to prevent burning. Simmer until translucent and cooked. Remove the naartjie peel and stick cinnamon just before serving.

Serves 6-8.

Pork roll with apricot and pecan nut stuffing

1,5-2 kg boned pork rib

115 ml wholegrain mustard

salt and freshly ground black pepper to taste

250 g soft dried apricots, finely chopped

150 g (1½ packets) Brazil nuts,
   toasted and chopped

60 ml (¼ c) chopped fresh parsley or sage

½ loaf white bread, crusts removed
   and crumbled

2 cloves garlic, finely chopped

150-200 ml soft butter or margarine

Preheat the oven to 160 °C (325 °F). With the meat side facing up, rub the mustard, salt and pepper into the meat. Mix the apricots, nuts, herbs, crumbs and garlic. Add the butter or margarine and mix to form a dry paste. Spread over the meat and roll up. Secure the roll with string and score the rind and fat, taking care not to slice through the meat.

Oven-roast the pork roll for 50 minutes per kilogram (about 1½ hours) plus an extra 25 minutes until the meat is done. Rest for 10 minutes, slice thinly and serve.

Serves 6-8.

Roast leg of lamb with herb sauce

60 ml (¼ c) finely chopped fresh rosemary
  and thyme
3 cloves garlic, finely chopped
salt and freshly ground black pepper to taste
100 ml olive oil
10 ml (2 t) paprika
10 ml (2 t) mustard powder
2,5 kg boned leg of lamb
  (reserve the fat and trimmings)

HERB SAUCE
30 ml (2 T) oil
2 small onions, finely chopped
5 allspice berries
10 coriander seeds
10 black peppercorns
250 ml (1 c) red wine
125 ml (½ c) port
small bunch rosemary and thyme
1 litre (4 c) quality mutton stock
cornflour
15 ml (1 T) butter

Preheat the oven to 200 °C (400 °F).

Combine the rosemary, thyme, garlic, salt and pepper, olive oil, paprika and mustard, and rub the mixture into the meat. Secure with string and set aside for about 2 hours.

Meanwhile, heat the oil in a heavy-based saucepan. Fry the fat and trimmings until golden brown. Add the onions, allspice, coriander and peppercorns and fry until the onions are translucent. Add the wine, port and herbs and reduce to a syrup consistency. Add the mutton stock and reduce by half. Thicken with a little cornflour, mixed with a litle water, and add 15 ml (1 T) butter. Keep warm.

Oven-roast the meat in the preheated oven for 15 minutes, reduce the heat to 160 °C (325 °F) and oven-roast for another 40 minutes per kilogram plus 20 minutes extra (about 1½-2 hours plus 20 minutes). Rest for about 15 minutes and serve with the sauce.

Serves 6-8.

Meringue towers with prickly pear cream

4 extra-large egg whites, at room temperature
pinch salt
250 ml (1 c) castor sugar
5 ml (1 t) vinegar
10 ml (2 t) cornflour
3 ripe prickly pears, peeled
500 ml (2 c) fresh cream, chilled
100 ml castor sugar
10 ml (2 t) vanilla essence

Preheat the oven to 140 °C (275 °F). Grease two baking sheets lightly with butter or margine or spray with nonstick spray and dust with cornflour. Mark circles in the cornflour using a glass about 7 cm in diameter.

Beat the egg whites and salt together until soft peaks form. Add the castor sugar by the spoonful, beating continuously. Beat until stiff and the mixture holds its shape. Fold in the vinegar and cornflour. Spoon the mixture into a piping bag and pipe flat circles on the patterns made on the baking sheets. Bake for about 35-40 minutes or until the meringues are dry and crisp. Switch off the oven and leave the meringue circles to cool in the oven.

Purée the ripe prickly pears in a food processor. Rub the purée through a sieve to remove the seeds. Whip the cream until stiff and fold in the castor sugar and vanilla essence. Just before serving, fold the prickly pear purée into the cream and chill.

Spoon a little of the cream onto a plate. Place a meringue circle on each plate and spoon a little of the cream mixture over the meringue. Repeat until there are three meringue layers. Decorate with fruit and prickly pear slices.

Serves 4-6.

Meringue towers with prickly pear cream

A few years ago, David and Lisa Donde settled on the only real farm left in Tokai. David took up poultry farming and Lisa, who has a law degree, decided to share her great love of cooking with others. David rebuilt the old barn himself, and converted it into their unique farm shop, the Barnyard, which boasts shelves fashioned from wood and sheets of metal. Lisa goes to a great deal of trouble when purchasing stock – all the products in their shop are home-made. Other specialities include cheeses and home-made ice creams, and in the fridge you may even find hummus, taramasalata and other exotic delicacies. Those in search of a breather can sit down to a cheese platter, bread and pâté, soup, or the hot meal of the day. Also on offer are cakes and muffins, to be enjoyed with a cup of excellent coffee. The Dondes have now opened a second Barnyard near Melkbos.

Whole-wheat loaf

Their bread is in great demand, says Lisa, and this whole-wheat loaf is always first to go. The dough requires no kneading.

1 kg white bread flour

800 g whole-wheat flour

50 ml brown sugar

2 packets (10 g each) instant yeast

125 ml (½ c) sunflower seeds

250 ml (1 c) oats

15 ml (1 T) salt

45 ml (3 T) oil

about 1,5 litres (6 c) lukewarm water

sesame and poppy seeds for sprinkling on top

Preheat the oven to 180 °C (350 °F). Grease one small and two large loaf tins with margarine or butter or spray with nonstick spray.

Place all the ingredients, except the sesame and poppy seeds, in a large mixing bowl and mix with the lukewarm water until the mixture is fairly slack, but does not stick to the sides of the bowl. Cover with plastic wrap and leave to rise for 20 minutes. Turn into the prepared tins and leave to rise again until the dough fills the tins. Sprinkle with the sesame and poppy seeds and bake for 25-35 minutes or until the bread sounds hollow when tapped. Turn out onto a wire rack to cool.

Serve with butter or chicken liver pâté.

Makes 2 large loaves and one small one.

Focaccia

This traditional Italian bread is a must with minestrone soup. The flavour can be adapted by kneading sun-dried tomatoes or olives with fried onions and a variety of freshly chopped herbs into the dough.

350 g white bread flour

2 ml (½ t) salt

10 ml (2 t) instant yeast

210 ml lukewarm water

15 ml (1 T) olive oil

a mixture of 8-10 sun-dried tomatoes,
  finely chopped; 1 chopped and fried
  onion; 50 ml chopped herbs

chopped garlic for sprinkling on top

Preheat the oven to 190 °C (375 °F). Grease two baking sheets well with butter or margarine or spray with nonstick spray.

Sift the flour and salt together into a large bowl. Sprinkle the instant yeast on top. Pour over the water and olive oil and add the herb mixture. Mix well and knead until the dough no longer sticks to your hands or the sides of the dish – about 10 minutes. Cover with plastic wrap and leave to rise in a warm place until doubled in volume. Punch down and divide in half. Shape each half into a ball, flatten slightly and make a cross on top of the dough with a knife. Sprinkle with a little olive oil and chopped herbs and garlic. Leave to rise again for about 30 minutes until doubled in volume. Bake for 20-25 minutes or until the bread is done or sounds hollow when tapped at the bottom.

Makes 2 loaves.

Spinach muffins

A Barnyard muffin is a meal in itself. We tested the recipe in shallower muffin pans and the recipe yielded a bigger batch.

6 x 250 ml (6 c) cake flour

45 ml (3 T) baking powder

15 ml (1 T) salt

10 ml (2 t) dried mixed herbs

750 ml (3 c) grated Cheddar cheese

2 bunches (300 g each) spinach,
  well rinsed, finely chopped, cooked
  and most of the liquid squeezed out

300 g margarine

250 ml (1 c) milk

250 ml (1 c) water

6 eggs, whisked

Preheat the oven to 180 °C (350 °F). Grease a few muffin pans with margarine or butter or spray with nonstick spray.

Sift the dry ingredients into a large mixing bowl. Add the cheese and spinach and mix. Melt the margarine and add with the remaining ingredients. Mix. Fill the hollows of the muffin pans three quarters full and bake for about 25 minutes or until done and a skewer comes out clean when inserted into the centre of the muffins.

Add a little extra water, about 100 ml, to the remaining dough if it has to wait until you make the next batch, as the mixture thickens while standing.

Makes 47 medium muffins.

Hummus

Hummus is a spread made from chickpeas. It goes beautifully with the spinach muffins.

250 ml (1 c) chickpeas,
  soaked in water overnight

2 cloves garlic, crushed

juice of 1 lemon

salt and freshly ground black pepper
  to taste

olive oil and paprika for sprinkling on top

Pour off the chickpea soaking water and boil the chickpeas in clean water until soft. Drain, but reserve about 125 ml (½ c) of the water. Mash with the 125 ml (½ c) water. Add the garlic, lemon juice and salt and pepper and mix to form a spread. Spoon into a dish and pour over a little olive oil. Sprinkle with paprika.

Makes about 500 ml (2 c).

Chicken liver pâté

1 container (250 g) chicken livers, cleaned

salt and pepper

225 g butter at room temperature

30 ml (2 T) brandy

15 ml (1 T) mustard powder

2 ml (¼ t) dried thyme

2 cloves garlic, crushed

Season the chicken livers to taste with salt and pepper. Melt 25 g of the butter and fry the chicken livers over medium heat until brown on the outside but still slightly pink inside. Remove from the pan and place in the food processor. Melt 150 g of the butter and add to the chicken livers. Add the brandy to the pan juices in the pan, mixing well. Add the mixture to the chicken livers in the food processor. Add seasonings and garlic.

Process until smooth and season with more salt and pepper if necessary. Spoon into a dish, melt the remaining butter and spoon on top. Chill until the butter has set.

Serve with the whole-wheat bread (p. 18).

Makes about 250 ml (1 c).

Minestrone

A deliciously thick soup made with vegetables and dried beans. Serve it with bread – focaccia is especially good with it – and Parmesan cheese for sprinkling on top.

1 small packet (500 g) sugar beans,
  soaked in hot water for 1 hour

50 ml margarine

30 ml (2 T) olive oil

2 medium onions, finely chopped

3 leeks, sliced into rings

4 stalks celery, finely chopped

1 bunch carrots, scraped clean
  and sliced into rings

1 bunch turnips, scraped clean
  and cut into pieces (optional)
  or 4-6 potatoes, peeled and cut into pieces

100 g green beans

350 g cabbage, finely shredded

15 ml (1 T) finely chopped garlic

3 litres (12 c) vegetable stock

5 ml (1 t) dried basil

1 tin (410 g) tomatoes, chopped

30 ml (2 T) tomato purée

250 g spaghetti, broken into smaller pieces

60 ml (¼ c) finely chopped parsley

salt and freshly ground black pepper to taste

Pour off the soaking water from the beans, cover with clean water and boil until soft. Drain and season with salt.

Heat the margarine and oil in a large saucepan and sauté all the fresh vegetables until glossy. Add the stock and drained beans, cover and simmer slowly for about 20 minutes. Add the dried basil, tomatoes, tomato purée and spaghetti and simmer slowly until the spaghetti is cooked and the soup is thick and flavoursome. Add the parsley and season to taste with salt and pepper.

Serves 8.

Sour-cream cheesecake

The sour-cream topping gives this cheesecake its unusual flavour. After testing the recipe, everyone at *You* wanted a copy.

CRUST

1 packet (200 g) Tennis biscuits, crushed

125 ml (½ c) butter, melted

FILLING

4 jumbo eggs

250 ml (1 c) sugar

60 ml (¼ c) lemon juice

3 tubs (250 g each) smooth cottage cheese

1 container (250 ml) cream

125 ml (½ c) cake flour

TOPPING

1 container (250 ml) sour cream

45 ml (3 T) castor sugar

5 ml (1 t) vanilla essence

Preheat the oven to 180 °C (350 °F). Grease a 23-cm loose-bottomed cake tin with butter or margarine or spray with non-stick spray.

Mix the crushed biscuits and butter and press onto the base of the prepared tin.

Whisk the eggs and sugar together until light and thick. Add the lemon juice while beating continuously. Add the cottage cheese, cream and cake flour and mix.

Turn the mixture into the prepared tin. Bake for 10 minutes, reduce the heat to 140 °C (275 °F) and bake for another hour or until the filling is firm, but slightly soft in the centre. Switch off the oven, but leave the cake inside to cool. Remove the cake from the tin when cold and transfer to a serving platter.

Mix all the ingredients for the topping and pour over the cake.

Makes a large cake.

From an early age, Heidi Vollmer dreamt of one day owning a coffee shop just as cosy and welcoming as the ones she had seen in Austria. A car accident during her final year of study left her partially paralysed, but did not dampen her enthusiasm. The fact that she was confined to a wheelchair became the strongest motivating force in her life. Forced to become more outspoken, self-motivated and positive, she learnt to assert herself and meet people's eyes unwaveringly, with a smile. She felt that by doing so she forced them to notice the person first, then the wheelchair. Heidi's Coffee Shop has been in operation for nearly ten years now. Healthy food is especially important to her and you will find the Heart Foundation logo next to some items on the menu .You can even order a "skinny cappuccino" made with skim milk.

Heidi has always been creative and enjoys making things by hand. For You she prepared a special New Year's feast which can be enjoyed anywhere, even on a yacht. Keep the food light, says Heidi. Fill plates with fresh ingredients, buy a variety of breads, make muffins and serve them with cheese. Cherries in the sparkling wine add to the festive feel, and salmon and attractive strawberry tartlets make the occasion special.

Smoked salmon on rye

Serve these snacks with the bubbly.

1 slice rye bread per person
a few thin slices cucumber
curly lettuce leaves
about 40 g smoked salmon per person
thinly sliced lemon
fresh dill for garnishing

Cut out bread circles using a cookie cutter. Arrange the cucumber slices in a circle on a side plate and place the bread and lettuce on top. Top with the smoked salmon, securing with a cocktail stick if necessary. Garnish with a rolled-up lemon slice and a sprig of dill.
    Serves 1.

Sparkling wine with cherries (top), smoked salmon on rye (middle) and Mediterranean summer platter (bottom)

Mediterranean summer platter

Line a large salad platter with a variety of lettuce leaves and fennel sprigs and top with a selection of the following:

whole cherry tomatoes

sun-dried tomatoes, soaked in olive oil

black calamata olives

gherkin slices

slices of Italian salami

feta cheese with black pepper, broken
  into pieces

Serve with olive bread, olive oil and freshly ground black pepper.

Smoked chicken salad with pineapple salsa

Assemble individual salads on plates, using a selection of the following ingredients, and serve with the salsa.

selection of salad leaves

smoked chicken breasts, thinly sliced

coarsely chopped tomato

cucumber slices

tinned pineapple rings, cut into pieces

coarsely chopped pecan nuts

olives

cherry tomatoes

fresh dill

SALSA

250 ml (1 c) olive oil

10 ml (2 t) pineapple juice

2 tinned pineapple rings

1 medium tomato

1 medium onion

1 sprig fresh dill

5 ml (1 t) finely chopped garlic

½ red chilli

salt and freshly ground black pepper

Process all the salsa ingredients in a food processor until well blended and season to taste. Serve with the chicken salad.

Makes about 300 ml salsa.

Variation: Use leftover smoked turkey or pork instead of the chicken.

Smoked chicken salad with pineapple salsa

Cheese muffins

500 ml (2 c) cake flour, sifted

12 ml (2½ t) baking powder

pinch salt and freshly ground black pepper

2 ml (½ t) mustard powder

500 ml (2 c) grated mature Cheddar cheese

1 medium onion, chopped

2 large cloves garlic, finely chopped

oil

10 ml (2 t) finely chopped fresh mixed herbs,
   or 5 ml (1 t) dried herbs

1 egg and milk

poppy seeds

Preheat the oven to 200 °C (400 °F). Grease two muffin pans with margarine or butter or spray with nonstick spray.

Sift the dry ingredients together and add the cheese. Sauté the onion and garlic in a little oil until tender and glossy. Add the herbs. Remove the pan from the heat and leave to cool. Beat the egg lightly and pour into a measuring cup. Add enough milk to make up about 300 ml. Add the onion and egg mixtures to the dry ingredients and stir until just well moistened. Spoon into the prepared muffin pans to three quarters full and sprinkle with the poppy seeds.

Bake for about 15-20 minutes until done and a skewer comes out clean when inserted in the centre of the muffins. Leave to cool in the muffin pans for 10 minutes before turning out. Cool until lukewarm and serve.

Makes about 10 large muffins.

Variation: Add chopped ham or bacon to make ham and cheese muffins.

Fresh strawberry tartlets

Bake the tartlet cases in advance and store them in an airtight container until needed.

SHORT-CRUST PASTRY

430 ml cake flour

pinch salt

70 ml (4 T + 2 t) castor sugar

125 g cold butter

2 extra-large egg yolks

about 10-15 ml (2-3 t) sour cream

100 g milk chocolate, broken into
   small pieces

CREAM FILLING

125 ml (½ c) cream

125 ml (½ c) plain yoghurt

castor sugar to taste

about 1 kg fresh strawberries, rinsed,
   hulled and halved

Sift the cake flour and salt together and add the castor sugar. Dice the butter and rub it into the flour with your fingertips until the mixture resembles fine breadcrumbs. Add the egg yolks and enough sour cream to form a soft pastry. Cover with plastic wrap and chill in the fridge for 30 minutes.

Preheat the oven to 200 °C (400 °F). Grease loose-bottomed tartlet tins, 6 cm in diameter, with margarine or butter or spray with nonstick spray.

Roll out the pastry thinly. Line the tartlet tins with pastry and cover with a sheet of wax paper. Fill the tins with dried beans or rice and bake for 10 minutes. Remove the beans and wax paper and bake the tartlet cases for another 3-4 minutes until done.

Remove from the oven and cool completely. Melt the chocolate in a glass bowl over boiling water or in the microwave oven. Dip the sides of the pastry cases into the melted chocolate and set aside.

Whip the cream for the filling until stiff and fold in the yoghurt. Sweeten with castor sugar to taste and spoon a little of the filling into each pastry case.

Arrange the strawberries on top and garnish with fresh herb flowers or mint leaves.

Makes about 24 tartlets.

Cheese muffins (left) and fresh strawberry tartlets (on the right)

Half an hour; that is all the time she needs to prepare a meal for friends, Marietjie Koekemoer assures us. In her cosy home in Protea Valley near Cape Town there are several tables at which guests can savour delicious food and chat to their hearts' content. The food is simple and natural, wholesome and healthy, without ostentation – new-style boerekos, served with great flair by this one-time Karoo girl.

Creamy tomato soup

2 large onions, chopped

2 large potatoes, cut into pieces

oil

6-8 large, ripe tomatoes, chopped

10 ml (2 t) vegetable stock powder,
    dissolved in 375 ml (1½ c)
    boiling water

a few fresh basil leaves

cream (optional)

Fry the onions and potatoes in a little oil for about 5 minutes until browned. Add the tomatoes and reduce the heat. Add the vegetable stock, cover and simmer until very tender. Pour the soup through a colander, retaining the liquid. Purée the vegetables and add a few basil leaves to taste. Return the purée and liquid to the saucepan and simmer until heated through.

Garnish with fresh basil and a small dollop of cream, if preferred. Serve hot or cold.

Serves 4.

Tasty fried baby chickens

baby chickens (1 per person)

MARINADE
garlic

fresh sage leaves or thyme

olive oil

balsamic vinegar

freshly ground black pepper

whole garlic bulbs

small onions

white wine

Remove all string from the baby chickens. Sprinkle a little chopped garlic and herbs over the chickens, followed by a sprinkling of olive oil and balsamic vinegar. Marinate the chickens for a few hours. Remove from the marinade and season with freshly ground black pepper.

Fry the baby chickens, a few whole garlic bulbs and some small onions on all sides in a little olive oil until golden brown. Reduce the heat and add a generous dash of white wine. Cover with the lid and simmer for about 20 minutes until done.

Rosemary pizza rolls

45 g (about 60 ml (¼ c))
    active dried yeast
    (not instant yeast)

300 ml lukewarm water

pinch salt

5 ml (1 t) olive oil

600 g (4⅓ c) white bread flour

sprigs fresh rosemary

coarse salt

Stir the yeast into the lukewarm water, add the salt and olive oil and leave until dissolved – about 10 minutes.

Place the flour in a mixing bowl and make a hollow in the centre. Pour the yeast mixture into the hollow drop by drop, incorporating the flour with your hands at the same time. Knead until smooth and shape into a ball. Cover with a cloth and leave to rise in a warm place until doubled in volume.

Gently punch down the risen dough and shape it into 10 small rolls. Flatten them gently with your hand to about 6 mm thick. Top with sprigs of fresh rosemary and sprinkle with coarse salt and a few drops of olive oil.

Heat an electric frying pan and add a drop of olive oil. Brown one roll on both sides, turning often until done. (Do not cover with the lid while the roll is browning.) The entire process takes about 5 minutes. Repeat with the remaining rolls.

Makes 10 rolls.

Tasty fried baby chickens

Melt-in-the-mouth venison

Serve fresh gooseberries and crushed wheat with this dish.

MARINADE
180 ml (¾ c) fresh lemon juice
20 ml (4 t) balsamic vinegar
60 ml (¼ c) olive oil
2 cloves garlic, crushed
3 lemon leaves
5 whole cloves
3 ml (generous ½ t) white pepper
10 ml (2 t) scorched and ground coriander

1,5 kg venison, e.g. springbok or sawn
  neck pieces
500 g lamb shanks or stewing lamb
250 g bacon, cut into pieces
2 medium onions, finely chopped
2 cloves garlic, crushed
375 ml (1½ c) water
salt to taste
250 ml (1 c) red wine
15 ml (1 T) cake flour
30 ml (2 T) quince jelly or smooth apricot jam
15 ml (1 T) natural yoghurt (optional)

Mix all the marinade ingredients and marinate the venison and lamb overnight.

Fry the bacon, onions and garlic in an open pressure cooker until the onions are tender. Add the marinated meat along with the marinade and water. Cover with the lid and pressure-cook for about 1½-2 hours or until the meat is tender and falling off the bones. Remove the lid when it is possible to do so. Transfer the meat to a large bowl and allow to cool.

Remove all the bones and mix the meat thoroughly. Season to taste with salt. Mix the red wine, flour and quince jelly or apricot jam to a paste and stir into the meat mixture. Transfer to a saucepan and heat through well. Remove from the heat and stir in the yoghurt, if preferred.

Spoon a little gravy onto a heated serving platter and stack the meat on top.

Serve with fresh gooseberries.

Serves 6-8.

Whole lamb shanks

This dish is a winner, served with mashed potatoes and a green salad. Squeeze the pulp from the garlic cloves and spread it over the meat.

4 whole lamb shanks
10 ml (2 t) olive oil
20 ml (4 t) balsamic vinegar
a few sprigs fresh rosemary
10 cloves garlic, unpeeled
4 small onions, unpeeled
1 tin (410 g) whole tomatoes
salt and freshly ground black pepper to taste

Sprinkle the lamb shanks with olive oil and vinegar, add the rosemary and garlic and marinate in the fridge overnight.

Brown the meat in a little olive oil. Add the marinade and the remaining ingredients, except the salt and black pepper. Cover with the lid and simmer for about 1 hour and 20 minutes until the meat is tender but still attached to the bones. Season with salt and pepper. Serve in a soup plate, on a bed of mashed potatoes. Surround with onions and garlic and pour the gravy over.

Serves 4.

Whole lamb shanks

Welcome to the
West Coast

Many tourists are fascinated by the West Coast with its icy waters, wind-swept beaches, harsh climate and sparse vegetation. Its attraction could be ascribed to the many faces it shows the world: though the scorching, merciless sun makes it almost a semidesert, the occasional fog not only brings welcome relief from the heat but also provides just enough moisture to make the wild flowers bloom in spring and transform the veld into a kaleidoscope of colours. I suspect, however, that the food and genial people of the West Coast are the real reason visitors return time after time. I know of several foreign guests – from Europe and even from Japan – who can't wait to visit Lamberts Bay again; to taste wind-dried bokkems and harders, West Coast snoek and crayfish fresh from the sea and grilled to juicy perfection over the coals, or piping hot farmhouse loaves straight from the Dutch oven, spread thickly with grape jam. Or perhaps it is the robust open-air eateries that brought fame to the West Coast.

It's very easy to overindulge at Bosduifklip, Muisbosskerm or Die Plaaskombuis near Lamberts Bay, because here you can feast on fish and seafood fresh from the sea, spit roasts and Sandveld country food with freshly baked bread and jam.

Muisbosskerm, the brainchild of Edward and Elmien Turner and probably the best known of all, was the very first open-air restaurant on the West Coast. One day Edward, who spent most of his waking hours beside the sea, built a muisbos windbreak for the times when he treated his friends to crayfish, braaied fish and all sorts of seafood. Later, he was persuaded to convert the shelter to a restaurant.

On the other side of the dirt road is Die Plaaskombuis, housed in the original clay-and-straw-walled farmhouse of the Burger family. Two tame crows welcome you as you step inside, where family portraits on the walls, oil lamps, oilcloths on the tables and Sandveld country food simmering in black, cast-iron pots on the wood-burning stove take you back to an earlier age.

At Bosduifklip, under the overhang where wood pigeons nest, guests dine at enormous blue gum tree stumps that serve as tables. A little further on are some ancient rock formations, rubbed smooth and shiny by elephants, centuries ago. Here you experience true country cuisine – from seafood to spit roasts, and even Ouma's souskluitjies.

At the end of 1999 we were invited to Saldanha's new landmark, the Blue Bay Lodge. The lodge, perched on the beach at Saldanha Bay, is luxurious in an understated way; it is open and spacious and radiates a stylish warmth. Cheerful blue gingham table cloths echo the ice blue of the sea; outside a fresh breeze ripples the water, and the strident cry of seagulls can be heard on the beach. Here you can revel in the warm hospitality of the West Coast and enjoy new-style homely fare – from land and sea – served with style.

At Die Plaaskombuis the menu is small, giving you a choice between a seafood or a tradi-tional Sandveld meal. Kitta Burger serves the food she grew up with, including pot-roast lamb from the farm, dune stew or green bean stew accompanied by deliciously sweet dried peaches, aniseed-flavoured sweet potatoes, pumpkin, rice and potatoes. Before the main course you're treated to flavoursome mussel soup and home-baked bread with farm butter, and koeksisters are served with the coffee.

Mussel soup

500 g frozen or tinned mussels

500 ml (2 c) water

60-100 ml butter

1 large onion, chopped

2 litres (8 c) longlife milk

2 chicken stock cubes

250 ml (1 c) cake flour

3 bay leaves

pinch dried origanum

25 ml (5 t) chopped fresh parsley

salt and freshly ground black pepper

250 ml (1 c) dry white wine

Place the mussels in a mixing bowl, pour over the water and set aside.

Heat the butter in a heavy-based saucepan and sauté the onion until soft. Heat the milk and stock cubes together. Sprinkle the flour over the onion and butter mixture, remove from the heat and gradually stir in the milk. Stir until smooth and return to the heat. Add the remaining ingredients, except the wine. Also add the mussels and water. Stir until the mixture comes to the boil. Simmer slowly until nice and flavoursome. Add the white wine and simmer for 5 minutes. Adjust the seasoning if necessary and serve hot.

Serves 10-12.

Farmhouse bread

8 x 250 ml (8 c) white bread flour

15 m l (1 T) salt

10 ml (2 t) instant yeast

30 ml (2 T) oil

15 ml (1 T) vinegar

about 600 ml lukewarm water

Lightly grease a deep 12 cm x 31 cm loaf tin with butter or margarine or spray with nonstick spray.

Mix the flour and salt in a large mixing bowl and add the yeast. Beat the oil, vinegar and water together and add to the yeast mixture. Mix to form a slightly slack dough and knead well until the dough no longer sticks to your hands.

Place the dough in the prepared loaf tin and leave to rise until doubled in volume.

Meanwhile, preheat the oven to 190 °C (375 °F).

Bake the bread for 1 hour until baked (the bread will sound hollow when tapped underneath.) Turn out and leave to cool.

Serve with mussel soup and farm butter.

Makes 1 large loaf.

At Bosduifklip you can eat either inside or alfresco – the choice is yours. In addition to baked and smoked snoek served with pot bread and griddlecakes – not to mention all the other delicious seafoods – Kobus Engelbrecht also roasts lamb on the spit, using his own secret method for getting tender, tasty results.

Aletta sees to the starters: marinated mussels, curried fish, or snoek pâté served with health bread.

Smoked snoek pâté

A delicacy from Bosduifklip – snoek pâté served with health bread.

750 ml (3 c) coarsely flaked smoked
  snoek

2 containers (250 g each) creamed
  cottage cheese

50 ml mayonnaise

½ medium onion, finely chopped

2-3 gherkins, finely chopped

30 ml (2 T) chopped fresh parsley

salt and freshly ground black pepper

Place all the ingredients in a food processor and process until smooth. Season to taste with salt and black pepper. Chill until firm. To make a coarser pâté mix the ingredients with a wooden spoon.

Makes about 4 cups of pâté.

Bosduifklip's baked snoek over the coals

Kobus Engelbrecht of Bosduifklip uses a butterflied, lightly salted snoek which he thaws in tap water if frozen. Melt about 30 ml (2 T) butter in a large stainless-steel pan and place the snoek in the pan, skin side down. Dot the thicker parts of the fish with butter, season with fish spice and lemon juice and cover with aluminium foil.

Bake slowly over the coals until all the butter has melted into the fish, by which time the fish should be ready, says Kobus.

Marinated mussels

1 kg frozen cooked mussels in half shells

MARINADE

15 ml (1 T) oil

60 ml (¼ c) vinegar

juice of 1 lemon

juice of 1 small orange

180 ml (¾ c) water

5 ml (1 t) balsamic vinegar

10 ml (2 t) sugar

pinch dried mixed herbs

10 ml (2 t) prepared mustard

salt and freshly ground black pepper

Thaw the mussels in tap water and drain.

Beat together all the ingredients for the marinade and pour over the mussels. Chill, preferably overnight, stirring occasionally.

Serve with bread.

Serves 6.

Curried fish

She first dips the fish in the curry sauce before rolling it in flour and frying it, says Aletta Engelbrecht of Bosduifklip.

SAUCE
15 ml (1 T) mild curry powder
2 ml (½ t) salt
5 ml (1 t) cornflour
15 ml (1 T) brown sugar
15 ml (1 T) vinegar
200 ml water

750 g hake, cut into portions
   and skinned
salt and pepper to taste
cake flour
oil for frying

Combine the dry ingredients for the sauce, add the remaining sauce ingredients and heat, stirring continuously, until the sauce comes to the boil and thickens slightly. Cool.

Season the fish with salt and pepper and dip in the curry sauce. Roll in cake flour and deep-fry in oil until golden brown and cooked. Layer the fish and sauce in a dish and serve.

Serves 6.

The Muisbos windbreak can still be seen next to the sea, looking nearly the same as it did when Edward Turner made it years ago for entertaining his friends. And today it's one of Lamberts Bay's attractions: people come from all over to indulge in braaied, baked and smoked fish served with green mealies, sweet potatoes and potatoes, as well as crayfish, when it's in season. Meat dishes include curried tripe and wild cabbage and waterblommetjie bredies (stews), and koeksisters are served with the coffee. Edward no longer goes there as often as he once did, but Elmien is just as busy as ever. She and her sons, Ian and Tertius, and the latter's wife, Elmarie, make the fires, pickle fish and onions, bake potato yeast bread in the Dutch oven and make sure that everyone has enough to eat.

Sauce for snoek

Even at the annual arts festival in Oudtshoorn, West Coast people braai snoek over the coals. The secret lies in the sauce, they say.

100 ml chutney
375 ml (1½ c) butter
10 ml (2 t) Worcester sauce
10 ml (2 t) oil
60 ml (¼ c) apricot jam
2 cloves garlic, crushed
75 ml (5 T) lemon juice

Heat all the ingredients together, except the lemon juice, and bring to the boil. Remove from the heat, stir in the lemon juice and brush the snoek with the sauce while it's braaiing.

Makes enough for 1 large snoek.

Braaied fish

At Muisbosskerm they braai all types of fish over the coals. When cooking fish over the coals, do not remove the scales, advises Tertius. Place whole, butterflied fish such as jakopewer, and fish steaks such as yellowtail on the grid and brush with lemon butter. Close the grid and grill slowly, turning often and brushing occasionally with lemon butter. Grill the fish skin side down during the last 10 minutes of the cooking time until cooked and succulent.

Harders

Harders are typical West Coast fare. Gut the harders by making an incision along the belly of the fish. Sprinkle coarse salt on the outside and place in a hinged grid. Grill slowly, turning often until cooked. The fish is done if the bones are slightly loose when you butterfly it, says Tertius.

Fried fish

At Muisbosskerm they dip fish fillets, such as hake, in lightly whisked egg and then in brown bread flour, says Elmarie Turner. Fry the fish in lots of oil until golden brown on the outside and cooked inside.

Seafood potjie

Add any seafood, e.g. fish, mussels or crayfish, depending on availability.

45 ml (3 T) butter

4 large onions, chopped

3 large cloves garlic, crushed

2 green sweet peppers, seeded and diced

250 g brown mushrooms, sliced

750 ml (3 c) uncooked long-grain rice

4 chicken stock cubes

8-9 x 250 ml (8-9 c) hot water

300 g fish such as hake or kabeljou, cubed

300 g frozen calamari or prawns

400 g frozen or tinned mussels

salt and lemon pepper

60-80 ml (¼-⅓ c) white wine

Melt the butter in a large, deep heavy-based saucepan or black cast-iron pot and sauté the onions, garlic, sweet peppers and mushrooms over medium heat until soft. Add the rice and mix.

Dissolve the stock cubes in the water and add to the rice mixture. Bring to the boil and cook until the rice is nearly tender and most of the water has been absorbed. Add the seafood, mix lightly and simmer slowly until the seafood is done. Season with salt and plenty of lemon pepper and add the white wine. Simmer for 5 minutes, remove from the coals and serve.

Serves 10.

The old family home was a warm haven to many, and today Marianne Wicht continues the tradition, receiving guests at Blue Bay Lodge with genuine West Coast hospitality. She drew up the plans herself for converting the old farmhouse to the spacious, welcoming guesthouse it is today. A friend bought the furniture in Bali, and it was left in a barn for a year to acclimatise. Marianne does all the cooking for the guesthouse and also caters for other large functions. She enjoys experimenting with new flavours and has attended several cookery courses, including Ina Paarman's. When there is a large function to cater for, Adie Kotze helps with the baking: they bake anything from bread to delicious bagels and savoury rolls. A complimentary packet of home-made rusks, packed with fribre, is put in each room.

Tomato tartlets

SOUR-CREAM DOUGH

750 ml (3 c) cake flour

5 ml (1 t) salt

250 g unsalted butter

250 ml (1 c) sour cream

FILLING

6 even-sized tomatoes, halved horizontally

olive oil

freshly chopped mixed herbs

brown sugar

Sift the cake flour and salt together three times. Rub the butter into the mixture lightly so it remains slightly lumpy. Lightly knead and lift to mix. Add the sour cream and cut in with a knife until well blended. Cover with plastic wrap and chill overnight. Remove from the fridge an hour before use. Roll and fold the dough 4 to 5 times. Press out circles and line the hollows in a greased muffin pan with them. Chill. Line each case with a sheet of baking paper and fill with uncooked rice.

Preheat the oven to 200 °C (400 °F) and bake until the cases are done. Remove the baking paper and rice.

Arrange the tomatoes on a baking sheet and brush with olive oil. Sprinkle with herbs and brown sugar and bake for 30 minutes at 180 °C (350 °F).

Arrange the tomatoes in the baked crusts and bake for another 10 minutes.

Serve warm.

Makes 12 tartlets.

Tomato tartlets

Perlemoen in wine sauce

2-3 perlemoen, cleaned
30 ml (2 T) butter
2 cloves garlic, crushed
125 ml (½ c) white wine
30 ml (2 T) cornflour, mixed with a little milk
100 ml cream
grated rind and juice of 1 lemon
nutmeg, salt and pepper

Beat the perlemoen flesh with a meat mallet until tender. Cut into cubes. Heat the butter in a pan and fry the perlemoen with the garlic until golden brown.

Add the wine and simmer for about 10 minutes until tender. Stir the cornflour into the mixture. Bring to the boil. Add the cream and heat through. Season with the lemon rind and juice and a little nutmeg, salt and pepper.

Serve with brown rice.
Serves 4-6.

Greek leg of lamb

125 ml (½ c) olive oil

125 ml (½ c) meat marinade

3 cloves garlic, crushed

1 boned and butterflied leg of lamb

Mix the olive oil, marinade and garlic and marinate the meat overnight. Brown the meat quickly in a little heated oil to seal it.

Oven-roast for about 1¼ hours at 160 °C (325 °F) until done but still slightly pink inside.

Serve with yoghurt sauce (see below).

Serves 8.

Yoghurt sauce

250 ml (1 c) Greek yoghurt

15 ml (1 T) finely chopped garlic

45 ml (3 T) chopped fresh coriander (dhania)

10 ml (2 t) olive oil

Mix the ingredients and chill until needed. Serve with the Greek leg of lamb.

Oven-baked vegetables with cumin and mustard seeds

4 potatoes, cut into wedges

8 baby onions, skinned

salt and pepper

125 ml (½ c) orange juice

125 ml (½ c) vegetable stock

olive oil

10 ml (2 t) cumin seeds

15 ml (1 T) mustard seeds

6 carrots, scraped and cut into chunks

2 small cabbages, cut into chunks

Preheat the oven to 180 °C (350 °F).

Arrange the potatoes and onions in an ovenproof dish. Season to taste with salt and pepper. Mix the orange juice and stock and pour over the vegetables. Brush with olive oil. Sprinkle with the seeds and bake for 30 minutes. Add the carrots and cabbage and bake until the vegetables are soft but still slightly crisp.

Serve with the Greek leg of lamb (p. 41).

Serves 8.

Greek nut biscuits

250 g butter

70 ml (4 T + 2 t) castor sugar

500 ml (2 c) cake flour

2 ml (½ t) salt

10 ml (2 t) almond essence

100 g (1 packet) ground almonds

sifted icing sugar for coating

Preheat the oven to 160 °C (325 °F).

Mix the ingredients to form a smooth dough. Form walnut-sized balls and arrange on a baking sheet. Chill for 30 minutes.

Bake for half an hour until just done and still light in colour. Roll in sifted icing sugar while hot and cool on a wire rack.

Enjoy with coffee.

Makes 25-30.

Summer cheesecake

CRUST

90 g butter

225 ml cake flour

80 ml (⅓ c) chopped pecan nuts

FILLING

3 containers (250 g each) smooth
   cottage cheese

15 ml (1 T) finely grated orange rind

25 ml (5 t) cake flour

3 extra-large eggs

2 egg yolks

220 ml sugar

pinch salt

5 ml (1 t) vanilla essence

TOPPING

125 ml (½ c) cream, whipped

1 tin (410 g) mixed berries

5-10 ml (1-2 t) cornflour, mixed to a
   paste with a little water

Preheat the oven to 160 °C (325 °F). Grease a 20-cm loose-bottomed baking tin with butter or margarine or spray with nonstick spray.

Mix the butter and cake flour together, add about 15 ml (1 T) iced water and mix to form a dough. Press the dough onto the base and sides of the tin. Bake for about 12 minutes until just done. Allow to cool and sprinkle with the nuts.

Mix the ingredients for the filling and pour into the crust. Reduce the temperature to 100 °C (200 °F) and bake the cheesecake for 1½ hours until just done. Turn off the oven and allow to cool in the oven. Chill until needed.

Spread the cream over the filling. Thicken the berry canning sauce with the cornflour paste by boiling them together, mix with the berries and spoon over the cream.

Makes a medium-sized cheesecake.

Whenever my colleagues and I feel the need to break away for a carefree seaside weekend, we make a beeline for Saldanha. This time we stayed in a small stone cottage among the dunes, where we could hear the waves breaking on the shore – and the cooking was simplicity itself.

Muesli with fruit and yoghurt

7 x 250 ml (7 c) oats

250 ml (1 c) sunflower seeds

250 ml (1 c) sesame seeds

250 ml (1 c) chopped almonds
   or other nuts

250 ml (1 c) desiccated coconut

250 ml (1 c) bran

2 ml (½ t) salt

250 ml (1 c) oil

250 ml (1 c) hot water

200 ml honey

5 ml (1 t) vanilla essence

250 ml (1 c) seedless raisins

Preheat the oven to 140 °C (275 °F).

Mix the dry ingredients in a large mixing bowl. Mix the oil, water, honey and vanilla essence and add to the dry ingredients. Mix well and spoon onto two baking sheets, spreading out evenly.

Bake for about 1 hour until pale brown. (Stir occasionally and check frequently that the mixture doesn't burn.) Allow to cool completely, turn into a mixing bowl and add the raisins. Mix and store in an airtight container. Serve for breakfast with yoghurt and stewed fruit or fresh fruit salad.

Makes about 14 cups of muesli.

Greek nut balls

French bread bake

Prepare everything the night before so it's ready to put in the oven the next morning. The dish is deliciously crisp on the outside and creamy inside.

1 long French loaf, cut diagonally
   into 1-cm thick slices
soft butter
750 ml (3 c) milk
3 extra-large eggs, whisked
salt and freshly ground black pepper
125 g (½ packet) streaky bacon
maple syrup or honey to taste

Butter the bread lightly and arrange in neat layers in a medium-sized, greased ovenproof dish. Beat the milk, eggs and seasoning together well and carefully pour over the bread. Cover and leave overnight to soak.

The next morning, preheat the oven to 180 °C (350 °F). Coarsely chop the bacon and sprinkle over the bread. Bake for about 30 minutes, drizzle generously with the maple syrup and continue baking until the top is crisp and brown. Allow to cool slightly and serve with more syrup if preferred.

Serves 4-6.

Ring the changes with braaied sosaties and serve them with vegetable parcels and braaied polenta slices.

Pork sosaties

The longer the sosaties are left to marinate, the better the taste.

4 pork schnitzels or leg of pork,
   cubed
1 packet (250 g) dried apricots
1 tin (440 g) pineapple pieces
juice of 2 oranges
30 ml (2 T) fruity chutney
15 ml (1 T) wholegrain mustard
10 ml (2 t) honey
15 ml (1 T) chopped fresh rosemary
salt and freshly ground black pepper

Thread the pork cubes onto skewers, alternating them with the apricots and pineapple pieces. Mix the rest of the ingredients, except the salt and pepper. Pour into a plastic or glass bowl and marinate the sosaties in the mixture. Season the sosaties with salt and pepper just before braaiing. Braai over medium coals until just done, basting often with the rest of the marinade.

Serves 4.

Tandoori chicken sosaties

The spicy chicken on a skewer is really delicious. The lemon wedges in between the chicken pieces not only look appetising – they also help to make the meat juicy and tender.

6 chicken breasts, skinned and boned
180 ml (¾ c) plain yoghurt
2 cloves garlic, crushed
45 ml (3 T) mild curry paste
15 ml (1 T) lemon juice
2 small, ripe lemons, cut into wedges

Slice the chicken breasts into fairly thin strips. Mix the yoghurt, garlic, curry paste and lemon juice together and marinate the chicken in the mixture, preferably overnight. Thread the chicken strips onto the skewers snake-style, alternating each strip with a lemon wedge. Braai over slow coals until just done and serve immediately.

Serves 4-6.

Pork sosaties and Tandoori chicken sosaties with vegetable parcels (p. 49) and braaied polenta slices (p. 48)

Paella with salad

60 ml (¼ c) olive oil

2 cloves garlic, crushed

1 medium onion, coarsely chopped

1 red sweet pepper, seeded and finely chopped

2 large chicken breasts, skinned,
  boned and diced

1 tin (400 g) whole tomatoes in juice,
  coarsely chopped

pinch chilli powder (or to taste)

5 ml (1 t) paprika

300 g uncooked long-grain white rice

1,3 litres vegetable stock

salt and freshly ground black pepper to taste

12 frozen prawns, unshelled

45 ml (3 T) sweet sherry

125 ml (½ c) frozen peas

1 tin (500 g) mussels in shells, drained

1 lemon, cut into wedges

handful fresh dill or parsley sprigs

Heat the olive oil in a large heavy-based saucepan or paella pan. Sauté the garlic, onion and sweet pepper until soft and fragrant. Add the chicken and fry until lightly browned. Add the tomatoes and stir. Sprinkle with the chilli powder and paprika, reduce the heat and simmer for about 10 minutes, stirring continuously. Add the rice, stir through and simmer for another 5 minutes.

Add the stock and bring to the boil. Reduce the heat and simmer uncovered until the rice is cooked and most of the liquid has been absorbed. Season to taste with salt and pepper. Meanwhile, shell the prawns and remove the alimentary canal.

Add the prawns, sherry and peas to the saucepan and simmer for another 5-10 minutes until the prawns are pink and just done. Arrange the mussels on top of the rice mixture, cover with a tight-fitting lid and simmer for 2-3 minutes until the mussels are heated through.

Serve the paella with lemon wedges and garnish with chopped dill or parsley. Prepare a simple salad with lettuce leaves, baby carrots, onion rings and tomato, drizzle with salad dressing and serve with the paella.

Serves 4-6.

Seafood soup

A quick recipe using tinned soup.

125 g (½ packet) streaky bacon, shredded

2 medium onions, finely chopped

3 stalks celery, finely chopped

2 leeks, sliced into thin rings

2 cloves garlic, crushed

3 medium potatoes, peeled and cubed

500 ml (2 c) chicken stock

500 ml (2 c) water

1 tin (425 g) seafood soup

500 ml (2 c) milk

500 g haddock fillets, cubed

10 ml (2 t) Worcester sauce

salt and freshly ground black pepper to taste

finely grated lemon rind

45 ml (3 T) finely chopped fresh parsley

50 ml cream

fresh dill or fennel

Fry the bacon in a large heavy-based saucepan until done. Add the onions, celery, leeks and garlic, and stir-fry until tender and fragrant. Meanwhile, cook the potato cubes in the chicken stock and water until just tender. Add the potatoes and stock to the bacon and vegetables in the heavy-based saucepan. Add the tinned seafood soup along with the milk and haddock. Heat until the mixture comes to the boil and the fish flakes easily with a fork. Simmer slowly for another 3 minutes until the soup has thickened slightly and tastes done. Season with Worcester sauce, salt and black pepper, lemon rind and chopped parsley. Pour into soup bowls or mugs and stir a spoon of cream into each serving. Garnish with fresh dill or fennel and serve with toasted French bread.

Serves 6.

Braaied polenta slices

Nowadays even packets of ready-cooked mealie meal porridge are available in the shops.

Use packets of ready-cooked polenta (Ezee-pap) and cut into neat slices. Brush the slices with olive oil and braai over the coals until lightly browned and crisp on the outside. Serve hot with the meat and vegetables.

Mini-loaves in a tin

Basic beer bread batter is baked in tins so there's a mini-loaf for each person.

1 kg (1 medium packet)
  self-raising flour
10 ml (2 t) salt
2 cans (2 x 340 ml) beer

Preheat the oven to 190 °C (375 °F). Grease 6 empty tins (410-g size) well with butter or margarine or spray with nonstick spray.

Sift the self-raising flour and salt together. Add the beer and mix well with a wooden spoon. Divide the dough into 6 equal parts and turn into the prepared tins.

Bake the loaves for about 30 minutes until nicely risen and done. Allow to cool slightly, turn out onto a wire rack and leave to cool completely. Use a knife to loosen the loaves slightly before turning out.

Serve with butter and cheese.

Vegetable parcels

1 large butternut, sliced into wedges

1 red sweet pepper, seeded and sliced
   into strips

1 green sweet pepper, seeded and sliced
   into strips

250 g (1 packet) brown mushrooms, sliced
   into thick strips

1 container baby corn, cut into pieces

10 courgettes, sliced into chunks

4 whole garlic bulbs, tops removed

olive oil

lemon juice

butter

salt and freshly ground black pepper to taste

Microwave or steam the butternut wedges and sweet pepper strips for a few minutes until slightly tender. Arrange the vegetables on a large piece of heavy-duty aluminium foil and baste with olive oil and lemon juice. Dot with knobs of butter and season with salt and pepper. Wrap the vegetables in the aluminium foil and wrap the parcel in another three layers of foil. Place the parcel among medium-hot coals and turn occasionally. Check if the vegetables are done after about 20-30 minutes.

Serves 6.

Marshmallow cookies

Marshmallows toasted over the coals make a delicious sweet treat after the meal.

1 packet white and pink marshmallows

1 packet Marie biscuits

kebab skewers

Thread a marshmallow onto a skewer and toast it over the coals until soft and brown. Use a fork to remove it from the skewer and sandwich it between two Marie biscuits. Allow to cool and serve with coffee.

White lamingtons

These delicious lamingtons are coated with white instead of dark chocolate sauce and taste a bit like coconut ice. If you're running late, buy a ready-made cake.

CAKE

375 ml (1½ c) white sugar

4 extra-large eggs

250 ml (1 c) milk

75 ml (5 T) sunflower oil

500 ml (2 c) cake flour

20 ml (4 t) baking powder

1 ml (¼ t) salt

5 ml (1 t) vanilla essence

ICING

350 g white chocolate, broken into squares

350 ml cream

about 30 ml (2 T) plain yoghurt

300 g desiccated coconut for rolling

Preheat the oven to 180 °C (350 °F). Grease a 33 cm x 27 cm x 5 cm oven pan well with butter or margarine or spray with nonstick spray. Line with baking paper and grease this as well.

Beat the sugar and eggs together thoroughly until thick and light. Boil the milk and oil together. Add the boiling milk mixture to the egg mixture in a thin stream, beating the mixture as you pour. Sift the flour, baking powder and salt together. Fold into the egg mixture. Add the vanilla essence and mix lightly. Turn the batter into the pan and bake for about 25 minutes or until golden brown and baked through.

Allow the cake to cool in the pan before loosening the edges with a knife if necessary. Carefully turn the cake out onto a wire rack. Remove the paper and allow to cool completely. Cut the cake into squares.

Heat the chocolate and cream over very low heat until the mixture is smooth. Stir occasionally. Allow to cool to room temperature before cooling completely in the fridge. Using a wire whisk, beat until thick and light. Add the yoghurt and mix. Cover the cake squares with the icing, then roll in the coconut. Leave in the fridge to set.

Makes 22 lamingtons.

Leipoldt
country

From the summit of the Piekenierskloof Pass you have a panoramic view of the valley with its countless citrus orchards, the meandering Olifants River and, opposite, Sneeukop in the Cedarberg – often snow-capped after a cold snap – towers over it all. This area is renowned for its oranges and rooibos tea, but many people also remember it as the home of our famous poet and writer C. Louis Leipoldt. He spent his childhood in Clanwilliam, where his father was the local minister, and the town is once again hosting an annual Leipoldt festival – not only to learn more about literature but also to rediscover the beauty of the country of his youth, which he described so well in one of his poems:

'n Handvol gruis uit die Hantam –
My liewe lekker Hantam-wyk!
'n Handvol gruis en gedroogde blare,
Waboom-blare, ghnarrabos-blare!
Arm was ek gister, en nou is ek ryk.

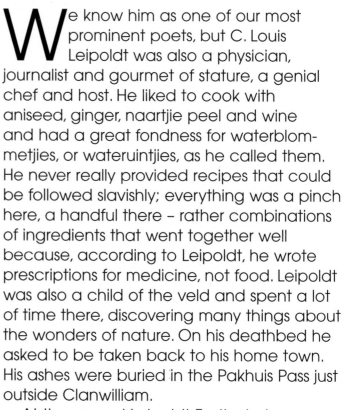

We know him as one of our most prominent poets, but C. Louis Leipoldt was also a physician, journalist and gourmet of stature, a genial chef and host. He liked to cook with aniseed, ginger, naartjie peel and wine and had a great fondness for waterblommetjies, or wateruintjies, as he called them. He never really provided recipes that could be followed slavishly; everything was a pinch here, a handful there – rather combinations of ingredients that went together well because, according to Leipoldt, he wrote prescriptions for medicine, not food. Leipoldt was also a child of the veld and spent a lot of time there, discovering many things about the wonders of nature. On his deathbed he asked to be taken back to his home town. His ashes were buried in the Pakhuis Pass just outside Clanwilliam.

At the annual Leipoldt Festival at Clanwilliam, at least one meal is planned according to Leipoldt's preferences. In the winter of 1998 we climbed a rocky hill outside the town to bring together Leipoldt's two great loves – food and nature.

At Olifantsrus, just outside Citrusdal, the foods of the region are in great demand. Regularly featured on the menu are snoek and orange-flavoured sweet potatoes, and bobotie with yellow rice, each accompanied by a brief history.

In these recipes you will find the flavours of naartjie peel and orange, ginger and aniseed – and there is also an old-fashioned chicken pie.

The Strassberger Hotel in Clanwilliam caters the Leipoldt meal each year. The hotel is renowned for its delicious country meals, and the Sunday lunch buffet is particularly popular. The Strassbergers have deep roots in Clanwilliam. Their grandfather was a missionary at Wupperthal, and today Ilse Lochner and her husband, Flip, run the hotel while her brother, Emile, manages Reinhold's Restaurant and Nancy's Tearoom.

Spinach loaf

A delicious dish combining two of Leipoldt's recipes.

1 bunch (300 g) spinach, stems removed, and well rinsed

3 small onions, chopped

3 cloves garlic, crushed

oil

50 g mature Cheddar cheese, grated

50 g dried white breadcrumbs

250 ml (1 c) thick cream

3 large eggs, whisked

5 ml (1 t) freshly grated nutmeg

10 ml (2 t) soy sauce

5 ml (1 t) ground ginger

5 ml (1 t) freshly ground black pepper

Preheat the oven to 180 °C (350 °F). Line a small loaf tin with butter paper and spray with nonstick spray.

Shred the spinach. Stir-fry the onions and garlic in heated oil until tender. Add the spinach and stir-fry. Remove from the heat. Stir in the cheese, breadcrumbs, cream and eggs. Process in the food processor until smooth. Add the seasonings and turn into the prepared loaf tin. Place the tin in an oven pan filled halfway with boiling water.

Bake for 1½ hours or until a skewer comes out clean when inserted in the centre of the loaf. Cool slightly, unmould and slice.

Makes 1 small loaf.

Aniseed rice

50 ml oil

1 large onion, chopped

½ green sweet pepper, seeded and finely chopped (optional)

½ red sweet pepper, seeded and finely chopped (optional)

5 ml (1 t) aniseed

375 ml (1½ c) uncooked rice

1 litre (4 c) boiling water

7 ml (1½ t) salt

Heat the oil and stir-fry the onion, sweet peppers and aniseed until the vegetables are tender. Add the rice and stir until covered with the vegetable mixture. Add the boiling water and salt, cover, reduce the heat and simmer until the rice is tender and done.

Serves 6.

Chicken roll with dried fruit

It requires quite a bit of skill to bone a chicken, which is why we boned the breast cavity only and filled it with the stuffing.

1 whole chicken
salt and pepper

STUFFING
150 g chicken fillet, finely chopped
2 ml (½ t) salt
3 ml (generous ½ t) fresh mixed herbs
1 large clove garlic, crushed
peel of 1 naartjie, grated
2 eggs, beaten
80 ml (⅓ c) cream
250 g dried peaches, boiled until soft
  with naartjie peel and 25 ml (5 t) sugar

Preheat the oven to 160 °C (325 °F).

Bone only the breast cavity of the chicken: With the breast facing up, cut through the breastbone. Press open and cut along the side of the ribs to remove. Season with salt and pepper to taste.

Mix all the ingredients for the stuffing, except the peaches, in a food processor and process. Spread on the inside of the chicken cavity and arrange the peaches on top. Secure the opening with cocktail sticks and place the chicken in an oven pan. Bake for about 1 hour or until the chicken is done and brown on the outside. Serve with aniseed rice (p. 53), orange-honey sweet potatoes and spinach loaf (p. 53).

Serves 4-6.

Sorghum bake

A meatless dish made with beans, sorghum and brinjals.

150 g dried beans, soaked

200 g sorghum

1 medium onion, chopped

1 red or green sweet pepper, seeded and chopped

15 ml (1 T) dried mixed herbs

5 ml (1 t) salt

3 ml (generous ½ t) freshly ground black pepper

1 large brinjal, sliced

oil

TOPPING

500 ml (2 c) plain yoghurt

10 ml (2 t) crushed garlic

10 ml (2 t) mustard powder

500 ml (2 c) grated Cheddar cheese

5 ml (1 t) salt

5 ml (1 t) cayenne pepper

Preheat the oven to 180 °C (350 °F). Grease a large oven dish with butter or margarine or spray with non-stick spray.

Boil the beans in fresh water until tender. Add the sorghum and another 600 ml water along with the onion, sweet pepper, herbs, salt and black pepper. Boil until tender.

Sprinkle the brinjal with salt and leave in a colander for about 15 minutes. Pat dry with paper towelling and fry in oil. Arrange a layer of brinjal in the bottom of the prepared dish. Spoon some of the bean mixture on top and repeat the layers.

Beat together all the ingredients for the topping and pour on top, letting it run into the mixture. Bake for about 20-30 minutes until golden brown. Serve hot.

Serves 8.

Ginger pudding

The pudding is made without eggs and forms its own sauce in the bottom of the dish. Serve with custard.

SAUCE

750 ml (3 c) sugar

1,25 litres (5 c) boiling water

12,5 ml (2½ t) lemon juice or vinegar

PUDDING

250 g soft margarine

100 ml apricot jam

125 ml (½ c) sugar

25 ml (5 t) bicarbonate of soda, dissolved in
　12,5 ml (2½ t) vinegar or lemon juice

750 ml (3 c) cake flour

10 ml (2 t) ground ginger

7 ml (1½ t) ground cinnamon

5 ml (1 t) salt

375 ml (1½ c) milk

Preheat the oven to 180 °C (350 °F). Grease a large oven pan well with butter or margarine or spray with nonstick spray.

Blend all the ingredients for the sauce and heat until the sugar has dissolved. Pour into the oven pan.

Beat together the margarine, apricot jam and sugar in a mixing bowl until well blended. Add the bicarbonate of soda and mix.

Sift together the dry ingredients and add to the margarine mixture, alternating with the milk. Mix and spoon into the prepared pan. Bake for 1 hour or until the pudding is done and a skewer comes out clean when inserted in the centre of the pudding.

Makes a large pudding.

Slices of chicken roll with dried fruit served with aniseed rice (p. 53), orange-honey sweet potatoes and spinach loaf (p. 53)

Chicken pie with rosemary crust

Serve the chicken pie with savoury rice, waterblommetjies and aniseed carrots.

CRUST

500 g cold butter

500 g cake flour

5 ml (1 t) chopped fresh rosemary

pinch salt

FILLING

1 medium onion, chopped

250 g mushrooms, sliced

oil

2 large carrots, scraped and cut into pieces

1 cooked chicken, boned and shredded

juice and finely grated rind of 2 lemons

500 ml (2 c) chicken stock

salt and freshly ground black pepper
  to taste

15 ml (1 T) cake flour

whisked egg yolk for brushing on top

Preheat the oven to 200 °C (400 °F). Grease a fairly large oven dish with butter or margarine or spray with nonstick spray.

Grate the butter into the cake flour and rub with your fingertips until well blended and the mixture resembles coarse breadcrumbs. Add the rosemary and salt, press the pastry together and shape into a ball. Chill until needed.

Sauté the onion and mushrooms in a little oil until tender. Add the carrots, shredded chicken, lemon juice and rind, and chicken stock and simmer for about 15 minutes until the carrots are tender and the flavours well blended. Season to taste with salt and pepper and thicken the sauce slightly with cake flour blended to a paste with a little water. Allow to cool.

Turn the mixture into the prepared oven dish and brush the sides of the dish with water.

Roll out the pastry and place over the filling. Pierce the pastry to allow the steam to escape. Brush with egg yolk and decorate with patterns cut from the remaining pastry. Bake for about 20 minutes or until the pastry is golden brown and done and the filling hot.

Serves 6-8.

Orange pudding with preserve

PUDDING

375 ml (1½ c) coarse-cut marmalade
   or kumquat preserve

5 extra-large eggs

250 ml (1 c) sugar

250 ml (1 c) milk

125 ml (½ c) butter

finely grated rind of 1 orange

500 ml (2 c) cake flour

10 ml (2 t) baking powder

5 ml (1 t) salt

SAUCE

500 ml (2 c) sugar

250 ml (1 c) water

30 ml (2 T) butter

250 ml (1 c) orange juice

5 ml (1 t) finely grated orange rind

Preheat the oven to 180 °C (350 °F). Grease an oven pan with butter or margarine or spray with nonstick spray.

Dot the bottom of the pan with knobs of marmalade. Whisk the eggs and sugar together very well. Heat the milk, butter and orange rind together until the butter has melted. Sift the remaining ingredients together and fold into the egg mixture, alternating with the milk mixture. Spoon into the pan and bake for 40 minutes or until a skewer comes out clean when inserted into the centre of the pudding.

Meanwhile, heat the sugar, water and butter together until the sugar has dissolved. Boil for 5 minutes and add the orange juice and rind. Make a few holes in the hot pudding and pour the sauce over.

Serve with ice cream and extra preserve, if preferred.

Makes a large pudding.

When you see the church steeple, you know you're nearing Citrusdal. But if you're travelling to Olifantsrus, take the Die Bad turnoff before you reach the town. Visitors to Olifantsrus are overwhelmed by the scenic beauty and the peace – and by the fact that they can pick fruit from a tree and take the dogs for a walk. But it's the perfectly prepared food they remember best of all about this place, where they arrive as guests and leave as friends. The hostess, Franci van Zyl, likes to serve traditional dishes, especially those indigenous to the region. The salad greens come from her garden and herbs grow all over the place. Desserts are her favourite and she enjoys trying new recipes.

Carrot and orange soup

The orange gives this creamy soup a wonderful flavour.

25 ml (5 t) butter
400 g carrots, scraped and cubed
1 large onion, chopped
750 ml (3 c) chicken stock
350 ml orange or tangelo juice
sugar, salt and pepper to taste
125 ml (½ c) cream (optional)
orange slices and chopped chives
   to garnish

Place the butter, carrots and onion in a saucepan and heat slowly. Cover with wax paper and allow to sweat for 5 minutes. Remove the wax paper, add the chicken stock and simmer slowly until the vegetables are tender. Process in a food processor until smooth or press through a fine sieve. Reheat in a clean saucepan and add the orange or tangelo juice, and sugar, salt and pepper to taste.

Add the cream just before serving and garnish with swirls of cream, orange slices and chopped chives. Serve hot or cold.

Serves 4.

Stuffed shoulder of lamb

The stuffing for this shoulder of lamb contains pieces of orange as well as pecan nuts.

1 boned shoulder of lamb
salt and freshly ground black pepper to taste

STUFFING
30 ml (2 T) butter
1 large onion, chopped
90 g fresh breadcrumbs
45 g sultanas
45 g raisins
90 g chopped pecan nuts
1 orange, cut into segments
15 ml (1 T) chopped fresh rosemary
10 ml (2 t) chopped fresh thyme
15 ml (1 T) finely crushed dried naartjie peel
  (without white membranes) or the grated
  rind of 1½ oranges
50 ml naartjie or orange juice

BASTING SAUCE
125 ml (½ c) red wine
300 ml lamb or beef stock
cornflour

GLAZE
60 g soft brown sugar
40 ml (8 t) lemon juice
40 ml (8 t) orange juice

Preheat the oven to 160 °C (325 °F).

Splay open the shoulder of lamb and season to taste with salt and pepper.

Melt the butter and sauté the onion until soft. Remove from the heat. Add the remaining stuffing ingredients and mix. Spoon onto the meat, roll up and secure with string. Place in a casserole dish, mix the ingredients for the basting sauce and pour over the meat. Cover and roast for about 1¼ hours or until tender, basting frequently.

Mix the glaze ingredients and brush over the meat 15 minutes before the end of roasting time. Keep the cover off and continue roasting.

Place the meat on a serving platter and keep warm in the warming drawer. Drain the fat from the dish. Add 125 ml (½ c) red wine to the pan juices and bring to the boil. Thicken with a little cornflour, mixed with a little water, and simmer until cooked.

Carve the shoulder into thin slices and serve with the hot gravy.

Serves 6.

Waterblommetjie phyllo parcels

Waterblommetjies are indigenous to this region and are excellent served with feta cheese in phyllo parcels.

FILLING
30 ml (2 T) butter
125 ml (½ c) chopped chives
250 g waterblommetjies, boiled and chopped
15 ml (1 T) lemon juice
2 extra-large eggs, lightly beaten
125 g feta cheese, crumbled
1 ml (¼ t) nutmeg
125 ml (½ c) dried breadcrumbs
salt and freshly ground black pepper to taste

10 sheets phyllo pastry, covered with a damp cloth
75 ml (5 T) butter, melted

Preheat the oven to 180 °C (350 °F). Grease a baking sheet with butter or margarine or spray with nonstick spray.

Melt the butter and sauté the chives until soft. Add the waterblommetjies and allow to cool slightly. Add the remaining filling ingredients and mix.

Brush one layer of phyllo pastry with melted butter and top with a second layer. Brush again with melted butter and slice lengthwise into four strips.

Spoon a tablespoonful of filling onto the pastry near one corner and fold diagonally to form a triangle. Keep folding until you reach the end of the pastry strip. It should look like a samoosa. Repeat with the remaining filling and pastry strips.

Place on the prepared baking sheet and brush again with melted butter. Bake for about 15 minutes until golden brown.

Arrange on a platter and decorate with salad leaves and olives. Sprinkle with a little olive oil and balsamic vinegar just before serving.

Makes 20 triangles.

Hint: Make the triangles the day before and chill until just before baking. The uncooked triangles can also be frozen. Thaw in the fridge, bake and serve.

Baked avocado with snoek

Smoked snoek and avocado are delicious together.

1 medium avocado
125 ml (½ c) creamy mayonnaise
125 ml (½ c) smoked snoek, flaked
freshly ground black pepper to taste
olive oil and balsamic vinegar

Preheat oven to 180 °C (350 °F).

Halve the avocado and remove the pip. Mix half the mayonnaise with the snoek and season generously with black pepper. Fill the avocado halves with the snoek mixture and top with the remaining mayonnaise.

Bake for about 10 minutes until warmed through and serve with mixed salad leaves and olives. Sprinkle with olive oil and balsamic vinegar.

Serves 2.

Baked avocado with snoek (right) and waterblommetjie phyllo parcels (far right)

Oven-baked snoek with citrus sauce

A hint of citrus peel in the sauce adds a delicious flavour.

75 ml (5 T) butter, melted

salt

60 ml (¼ c) fresh lemon juice

125 ml (½ c) mayonnaise

80 ml (⅓ c) smooth apricot jam

5 ml (1 t) finely crushed dried naartjie peel,
   white membranes removed

5 ml (1 t) grated fresh orange peel

1 medium-sized snoek

freshly ground black pepper

Preheat the oven to 180 °C (350 °F) and brush a large baking sheet with the melted butter. Lightly sprinkle fine salt over the butter and add half the lemon juice. Mix the mayonnaise, apricot jam and peel in a bowl.

Open the snoek out flat and make diagonal incisions across the width of the fish at 5-cm intervals. (Cut through the bones but not the skin.) Place the snoek on the prepared baking sheet, skin side down, and season with salt, black pepper and the remaining lemon juice. (Use a little or no salt if the snoek has been heavily presalted.) Bake for about 15 minutes until cooked. The fish should flake easily with a fork.

Spread the mayonnaise mixture over the snoek and grill for 10 minutes until the sauce starts to brown. Slide onto a serving platter and carefully cut open the incisions with a knife and fork to serve in neat portions.

Serve with oven-baked sweet potatoes.

Serves 6.

Pears in red wine

Franci says Goue Vallei pinotage, in particular, gives the pears a beautiful colour. She mixes natural yoghurt with the cream to make the mixture less rich and sweet.

6 small, firm pears, peeled, but stems retained

500 ml (2 c) red wine

250 ml (1 c) sugar

10-cm strip of lemon peel

1 cinnamon stick

3 whole cloves

5 ml (1 t) cornflour

YOGHURT MIXTURE

250 ml (1 c) cream, chilled

15 ml (1 T) icing sugar

5 ml (1 t) vanilla essence

250 ml (1 c) natural yoghurt

fresh mint to garnish

Core the pears with a small, sharp knife or vegetable peeler. Heat the wine, sugar, lemon peel, cinnamon and cloves together, stirring until the sugar has dissolved. Bring to the boil and place the pears in the boiling syrup. Reduce the heat slightly and simmer for 30-45 minutes until tender and done.

Using a slotted spoon, remove the pears and whole spices from the syrup. Set the pears aside. Mix the cornflour with a little water and stir into the syrup. Boil until cooked and glossy. Pour over the pears and allow to cool.

Just before serving: Whip the cream until stiff and fold in the icing sugar and vanilla essence. Stir in the yoghurt and place a spoonful of the mixture in each serving dish or glass. Place a pear on top and spoon a little syrup over. (Heat the syrup slightly if it is too thick.) Decorate with fresh mint and serve.

Serves 6.

Citrus-flavoured baked custard

The hint of orange makes this baked custard a special treat.

125 ml (½ c) sugar

125 ml (½ c) water

1 tin (397 g) condensed milk

250 ml (1 c) milk

15 ml (1 T) grated orange rind

2 extra-large eggs

2 egg yolks

5 ml (1 t) vanilla essence

Preheat the oven to 160 °C (325 °F) and heat 8 small glass dishes (ramekins) in the oven.

Heat the sugar and water, stirring until the sugar has dissolved. Bring to the boil and cook until a golden caramel colour is obtained. Do not stir. Remove from the stove and add 15 ml (1 T) hot water. Spoon a thin layer into each dish and set aside.

Mix the condensed milk, milk and orange rind and heat to just below boiling point. Remove from heat and allow to stand for 30 minutes for the orange flavour to develop.

Beat the eggs, egg yolks and vanilla essence together and beat in the cooled milk mixture. Strain the mixture through a fine sieve and divide between the glass dishes. Place the dishes in an oven pan filled halfway with boiling water. Carefully cover with a layer of aluminium foil. Bake for about 30 minutes until set. Remove from the water and allow to cool. Cover with plastic wrap and cool until just before serving.

Carefully loosen the edge of the custard with a knife and place the serving plate, right side down, on top. Invert the two dishes together, shaking the dessert slightly to unmould.

Decorate to taste and serve immediately after unmoulding.
Serves 8.

Cherry pavlova

Franci bottled the cherries for this pavlova herself, but tinned ones will also do.

MERINGUE

2 extra-large egg whites

pinch cream of tartar

125 g castor sugar

60 ml (¼ c) chopped pecan nuts

FILLING

1 tin (410 g) cherries

45 ml (3 T) cornflour

30 ml (2 T) cherry liqueur or brandy

YOGHURT MIXTURE

250 ml (1 c) cream, chilled

30 ml (2 T) icing sugar

5 ml (1 t) vanilla essence

30 ml (2 T) cherry liqueur or brandy

250 ml (1 c) natural yoghurt

fresh mint to decorate

Preheat the oven to 130 °C (260 °F). Line a baking sheet with wax paper and sift a little cornflour over the paper.

Beat the egg whites and cream of tartar together until stiff. Add 5 ml (1 t) castor sugar and beat again for a minute, then fold in the remaining castor sugar and the nuts. Place a spoonful of the mixture on the baking sheet, spreading it slightly, and make a slight hollow in the centre. Repeat until all the meringue mixture has been used and there are about 12 meringues on the baking sheet. Bake for about 1 hour until dry, cool in the oven and store in an airtight container.

To serve: Drain the cherry syrup into a saucepan and thicken with the cornflour. Bring to the boil, stirring continuously, and simmer until thick and glossy. Pour the liqueur over the cherries and leave for 30 minutes. Add to the syrup and allow to cool.

Whip the cream until stiff and fold in the icing sugar and vanilla essence. Flavour with the liqueur or brandy and fold in the yoghurt. Just before serving, place a large scoop of the yoghurt mixture in each meringue and spoon over some cherries and sauce. Decorate with fresh mint and serve immediately.
Serves 12.

Kalahari safari

In the Northern Cape, on the umbilical cord of South Africa, lies the town of Upington just where the Gariep loops in the Orange River valley. Here, genuine caring has not yet vanished, or, as Niel Stemmet says in his unique Kalahari Afrikaans: "In die Upington-dorp van ons leef jy met jou hart se deure oop, oorlat die wêreld hier by ons jou gebrei het tot die liefmens wat jy is." And it's also the Kalahari which inspired its very own Bettie van Niekerk to write this:

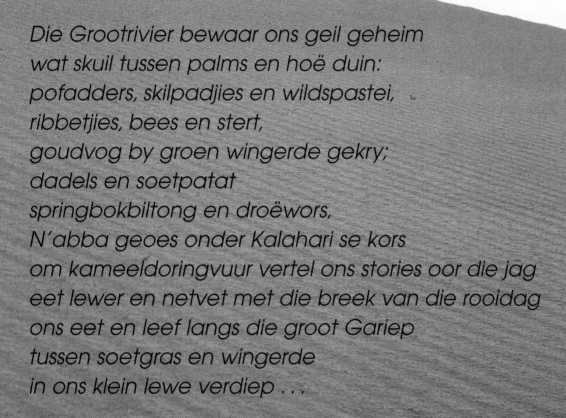

Die Grootrivier bewaar ons geil geheim
wat skuil tussen palms en hoë duin:
pofadders, skilpadjies en wildspastei,
ribbetjies, bees en stert,
goudvog by groen wingerde gekry;
dadels en soetpatat
springbokbiltong en droëwors,
N'abba geoes onder Kalahari se kors
om kameeldoringvuur vertel ons stories oor die jag
eet lewer en netvet met die breek van die rooidag
ons eet en leef langs die groot Gariep
tussen soetgras en wingerde
in ons klein lewe verdiep . . .

When the vineyards transform the Kalahari with splashes of green among the rocky hills, the people start to prepare for their festivals. First it was the Raisin Festival – after all, the best raisins and sultanas in the country originate here, along the banks of the Orange River. *You* has been visiting the Kalahari regularly ever since. At first we travelled all the way by train; later we were invited by Duineveld High School to participate in their Northern Cape chef's competition; and in 2000 we attended the first fully fledged Kalahari Kuierfees. The townspeople celebrated from early in the morning, when the hadedahs proclaimed the dawn, until late at night, when colonies of white herons moved downstream to find rest on the island. Concerts were held as in the old days; famous singers from all over the country came to make music and treated us to cabaret shows. Every night people rushed in from Raap en Skraap, Augrabies, Keimoes, Kakamas, Blouputs and Boegoeberg to queue for tickets and participate in this great cultural experience – the Kalahari Kuierfees.

And this is where I discovered real food at its very best. Here Niel Stemmet and his people have been serving magical food for years – everything improvised from basic ingredients, resulting in authentic, unembellished dishes. Le Must restaurant belongs to the people of Upington, not only to him, says Niel, the true food ambassador of the Kalahari who sees guests off with this wish: "We hope this meal has been like one in your mother's house. Go home, sleep with love and joy in your heart and please, please visit us again!"

Le Must is an institution in the heart of the Kalahari. The menu combines exotic dishes and our own traditional delicacies – real food prepared by the cook, Emily, and her staff of six. They have no formal training, just an instinct for flavours and colours which enables them to cook as only your mother could.

During our very first visit to the Raisin Festival we enjoyed an authentic Kalahari meal at Le Must. The following recipes were given to us by Niel Stemmet.

Biltong and blue-cheese muffins

5 extra-large eggs

500 ml (2 c) buttermilk

180 ml (¾ c) olive oil

500 g self-raising flour

750 ml (3 c) cake flour

10 ml (2 t) bicarbonate of soda

10 ml (2 t) baking powder

5 ml (1 t) salt

2 ml (½ t) paprika

250 ml (1 c) currants, soaked in port
  and water

500 ml (2 c) gemsbok biltong, chopped
  and soaked in dry sherry

500 ml (2 c) grated blue cheese

a few sprigs finely chopped fresh rosemary

Preheat the oven to 200 °C (400 °F). Grease muffin pans well with butter or margarine or spray with nonstick spray.

In a mixing bowl, beat together the eggs, buttermilk and oil with a wooden spoon. Add the remaining ingredients, mixing well.

Turn the batter into the pans, filling the hollows about three-quarters of the way. Bake for 20 minutes. Remove from the oven and spread with lashings of butter.

Serve with Marmite butter and real coffee.

Makes 45 muffins.

Smoked springbok and salad greens

Arrange fresh ingredients from your vegetable garden on a platter. Add the following: avocado sprinkled with lemon juice, spring onions, raisins soaked in port overnight and edible flowers. Intersperse the salad ingredients with slices of smoked springbok. Prepare the salad dressing using about 45 ml (3 T) olive oil, 10 ml (2 t) lemon juice, 5 ml (1 t) grape vinegar, 15 ml (1 T) freshly chopped basil, a few pieces lemon rind, 50 g crumbled feta cheese, about 15 ml (1 T) orange juice and 5 ml (1 t) sweet mustard. Heat gently and pour the mixture over the salad. Mop up the remaining salad dressing with a slice of fresh farmhouse bread.

Kalahari oysters chased with garlic

This dish is rich, so have your heartburn remedy ready. Grind a piece of sheep's liver coarsely and bind it with an egg and some oats. Season with rosemary, coriander, salt and ground pepper. Wrap the mixture in caul fat and braai over the coals, grill in the oven, or deep-fry. Serve with a green salad, a small scoop of prepared mustard and a little fried garlic. Invite all your neighbours and impress them with your Kalahari cuisine.

Niel's pumpkin with Bokkie's green figs

Prepare the pumpkin as usual, but add some yellow sugar and shredded preserved figs with their syrup. Turn into an ovenproof dish and grill until nicely browned. Remove from the oven, drizzle with farm cream – and forget about the kilojoules!

Kalahari mutton shanks

olive oil and butter

6 onions, sliced into rings

3 red sweet peppers, seeded and sliced into strips

3 green sweet peppers, seeded and sliced into strips

2 pieces (5 cm each) fresh ginger, chopped

1 sprig rosemary

6 cloves garlic, coarsely chopped

5 ml (1 t) each turmeric, masala, saffron and nutmeg

8 whole cloves

8 cinnamon sticks

45 ml (3 T) brown sugar

2,5 kg mutton shanks

seasoned flour

750 ml (3 c) hot meat stock

500 g mixed dried fruit

250 ml (1 c) chutney

30 ml (2 T) grated orange rind

salt and freshly ground black pepper

cold butter

apricot jam

orange slices and lemon thyme to garnish

Heat a little olive oil and butter in a black cast-iron pot. Sauté the vegetables until translucent and remove from the pot. In the same pot, fry the herbs, seasonings and sugar until the mixture caramelises. Remove from the pot.

Dredge the mutton shanks with the seasoned flour and fry, in the same pot, until brown all over. Add the vegetables and herbs to the pot, followed by the meat stock. Cover and simmer until the meat is nearly tender. Add the dried fruit, chutney and orange rind and simmer until the fruit is tender. Taste and adjust seasoning if necessary. Stir in a large knob of cold butter and a spoonful of apricot jam. Serve on a bed of white rice and surround with a few orange slices. Sprinkle with lemon thyme to add a bit of greenery.

The dish will easily serve 10 hungry mouths.

Slices of beef fillet with chicken livers

Clean a bowl of chicken livers and soak overnight in salted water. In a separate bowl, soak a handful of sultanas and dried peaches overnight in a mixture of port and water. The next morning, chop an onion and some garlic and sauté in farm butter until nearly translucent. Sprinkle with salt, freshly ground pepper, fresh rosemary and a dash of Tabasco. Add a handful of chopped bacon and fry until crisp. Add the chicken livers and fry until brown on the outside but still pink inside. Add a dash of mustard, followed by the sultanas and dried peaches. Mince and add the drained-off port and water as needed.

Grill the fillet according to your preference. Cover with the chicken liver sauce and open a bottle of good red wine that will do justice to a magnificent meal.

Pavlova

3 large egg whites

pinch salt

250 ml (1 c) castor sugar

15 ml (1 T) cornflour

10 ml (2 t) white vinegar

5 ml (1 t) vanilla essence

10 ml (2 t) freshly chopped garden-fresh
   geranium leaves (optional)

FILLING

250 g stoned prunes, soaked overnight in 125 ml
   (½ c) port and 125 ml (½ c) water

2 containers (250 g each) mascarpone cheese
   or cream cheese

3 generous tots Van der Hum liqueur

cream

toasted nuts (any kind, or mixed)

Preheat the oven to 140 °C (275 °F). Keep a baking sheet ready.

Whisk the egg whites with a pinch of salt until soft peaks form. Sprinkle small handfuls of sugar over the egg whites, beating well after each addition. Beat the mixture until very stiff peaks form. Using a metal spoon, gently fold in the cornflour, vinegar, vanilla essence and leaves.

Cover the baking sheet with aluminium foil, dust with a little cornflour and spread two-thirds of the mixture on the baking sheet, shaping it into a round base. Pipe the remaining meringue mixture along the circumference of the circle. Bake for about 1 hour (do not open the oven door). Switch off the oven and leave the meringue in the oven until it has cooled.

Make the filling: Drain the soaked prunes, reserve a few whole prunes for decoration, and liquidise the rest with the soaking liquid. Mix the mascarpone cheese with the liqueur. Fold the prune mixture into the cheese to create a marbled effect. Spoon the mascarpone mixture into the meringue hollow. Decorate with dollops of cream and the reserved whole prunes. Sprinkle with the toasted nuts. Add the finishing touches with an array of pretty blooms from the garden.

Serves 6.

During our 2000 visit, we encountered an entirely new menu, combining the latest food trends skilfully with Niel's beloved Kalahari foods.

He says he makes a point of asking guests how their product can be improved. Today the food is a showcase for the food culture of the Northwest. Niel always teaches his staff and the young people from the hotel and cookery schools to walk around in the veld and garden and to smell, look, touch and taste – and then to throw everything together in the kitchen without following recipes religiously.

Pan-fried fresh asparagus with lemon and Parmesan shavings

Use about 6 asparagus spears per person. Trim the hard ends of the asparagus. Heat a little butter in a pan and stir-fry the asparagus with a little lemon juice and thyme leaves until just done. (You can also stir-fry slices of fresh lemon with the asparagus.) Remove from the heat and place on a white plate. Season with a generous dash of balsamic vinegar and a few drops of olive oil. Scatter with Parmesan shavings (cut with a potato peeler). Dot with ready-made basil pesto and serve.

Roasted beetroot soup

A popular new addition to the menu.

10 young beetroot, scrubbed

2 onions, peeled and grated

3 carrots, scraped and grated

15 ml (1 T) butter

1 Granny Smith apple, peeled, cored
   and grated

1½ chicken stock cubes, dissolved in
   250 ml (1 c) boiling water

750 ml (3 c) water

750 ml (3 c) Bulgarian yoghurt

salt and freshly ground black pepper

cream

dill

Preheat the oven to 190 °C (375 °F). Wrap the beetroot in aluminium foil and bake for about an hour, or until tender. Remove the aluminium foil from the beetroot and allow to cool slightly. Skin the beetroot and grate coarsely.

Sauté the onions and carrots in the butter until tender. Add the beetroot, apple, chicken stock and water. Bring to the boil, reduce the heat and simmer slowly until the vegetables are tender. Remove from the heat, allow to cool slightly and process in a food processor until smooth. Stir in the yoghurt and season with salt and pepper. Stir in a spoonful of cream or plain yoghurt just before serving.

Garnish with dill if preferred.

Pumpkin and feta risotto

This is a personal favourite of mine.

500 g pumpkin or butternut, peeled and cubed

salt and freshly ground black pepper to taste

olive oil

RISOTTO

30 ml (2 T) olive oil

500 ml (2 c) Arborio rice

5 chicken or vegetable stock cubes,
   dissolved in 1,25 litres (5 c) hot water

TO FINISH

2-3 rounds feta cheese

Parmesan cheese

nutmeg

chopped spring onions

freshly ground black pepper

olive oil and balsamic vinegar

butter (optional)

Preheat the oven to 220 °C (425 °F). Arrange the pumpkin in a single layer in a buttered oven pan or dish. Season to taste with salt and black pepper and sprinkle with olive oil. Bake for about 20 minutes until tender.

Heat olive oil in a heavy-based saucepan, add the rice and stir-fry for about 1-2 minutes until glossy. Add 250 ml (1 c) of the stock and stir gently until all the liquid has been absorbed. Continue adding the rest of the stock by the cupful, stirring until absorbed and the rice has a creamy texture. Remove from the heat.

Mix the rice and pumpkin and add feta cheese to taste. Grate in a little Parmesan cheese and nutmeg to taste. Finish with chopped spring onions, freshly ground black pepper and a drizzle of olive and balsamic vinegar. Stir in a knob of butter for a creamier risotto.

Serves 4-6.

Pumpkin and feta risotto

In Niel's kitchen they like serving braised tomato sauce, potato cakes and roasted vegetables with the dishes. Deep-fried leeks or herbs are used as garnishes.

Braised tomato sauce

Braise 5 skinned fresh tomatoes until a thick sauce is formed. Season with salt, pepper and a pinch of sugar.

Potato cake

Boil an unpeeled potato until just tender. Mash the potato slightly with a spoon. Season with nutmeg, salt and pepper to taste and add chopped spring onions. Stir in a spoonful of the tomato sauce. Butter a fairly large cup and press the potato into the base to form a flat, round cake. Turn out onto a plate when needed.

Grilled and fried vegetables

Cut a selection of vegetables such as courgettes, brinjals, carrots, patty pans and cauliflower into long strips or slices. Heat a grilling pan until hot and pan-grill the vegetables until slightly charred. Heat together a little olive oil and a knob of butter in a heavy-based pan and sauté the vegetables until just done. Season with coarse salt and freshly ground black pepper.

Deep-fried leeks or spring onions

Wash the leeks well and cut into long, fairly thin but slightly chunky strips. Break the spring onions into stems, if used. Pat dry and deep-fry in hot oil until slightly tender. Drain and sprinkle generously with coarsely ground salt and black pepper. Also sprinkle with some balsamic vinegar.

Any herbs, such as sprigs of parsley, young beetroot leaves or spinach leaves, can also be deep-fried. Use these as garnishes.

These basic dishes can also be combined to make a delicious vegetarian meal. Do the following:

Turn a potato cake out onto a plate and top with grilled vegetables. Surround with a little braised tomato sauce and finish with deep-fried leeks if preferred. Sprinkle with balsamic vinegar and olive oil.

Serves 2.

Grilled rump steak with feta cheese and tomato

The people of the Kalahari enjoy meat. This is one of Le Must's signature dishes and Niel wouldn't dare leave it off the menu.

Season a large rump steak with mustard, balsamic vinegar and freshly ground black pepper. Spread with a little Marmite, if preferred, and grill over hot coals until just done to taste.

Meanwhile, preheat the oven to 200 °C (400 °F) and oven-roast a few tomatoes seasoned with fresh rosemary and whole cloves of garlic and drizzled with a little olive oil. When the meat is nearly done, grill a round of feta cheese until the cheese just begins to melt. Spoon a little braised tomato sauce (p. 76) on a plate and place the rump steak on top of the sauce. Top with the feta and finish with the oven-roasted tomatoes. A swirl of port sauce (see ostrich fillet, p. 78) adds the final touch.

Serves 1.

Kalahari lamb chops with brandy cream sauce

Kalahari chops are beautifully tender and tasty.

If preferred, clean the bones of the chops using a sharp knife. Pan-fry 2 lamb chops per person in a little olive oil until just done. Remove the chops and add a tot of brandy and half a beef stock cube to the pan. Add about 200 ml cream, bring to the boil, reduce the heat and simmer until the sauce is reduced by half. Serve the lamb chops on a potato cake (p. 76) with roasted vegetables (p. 76) and finish with deep-fried leeks (p. 76). Drizzle with the brandy and cream sauce.
   Serves 1.

Ostrich fillet with green figs and port sauce

Green figs filled with blue cheese complement the ostrich fillet perfectly.

250 g ostrich fillet

15 ml (1 T) balsamic vinegar

grated rind of 1 lemon

freshly ground black pepper

10 ml (2 t) olive oil

a fairly large piece blue cheese

1 whole preserved fig, halved

PORT SAUCE

250 ml (1 c) chicken stock

125 ml (½ c) port

5 ml (1 t) balsamic vinegar

3 ml (generous ½ t) green peppercorns

25 ml (5 t) cream

15 g butter

Preheat the oven to 220 °C (425 °F). Season the ostrich fillet with balsamic vinegar, lemon rind and black pepper. Heat the olive oil in a pan and seal the meat on all sides. Place the meat on a baking sheet and oven-roast until medium-done, about 7-10 minutes. Remove from the oven. Press the blue cheese into the hollows of the green fig halves and arrange on a baking sheet. Oven-grill until the cheese just begins to melt. Set aside.

Heat the chicken stock, port, balsamic vinegar and green peppercorns in a saucepan and reduce by about three-quarters. Add the cream and heat to just below boiling. Beat in the butter.

Slice the fillet and arrange on a plate. Pour over the sauce and place the grilled fig halves on the side. Serve with roasted red sweet peppers, asparagus and deep-fried leeks. (p. 76).

Makes 1 generous portion or 2 smaller portions.

Pork fillet in a pecan nut crust served with berry sauce

The nutty crust makes this dish outstanding.

300 g whole pork fillet
salt and freshly ground black pepper
40 ml (8 t) cake flour
50 ml milk
60 ml (¼ c) toasted pecan nuts, finely chopped
25 g butter
25 ml (5 t) olive oil
1 sprig lemon thyme

BERRY SAUCE
50 ml mixed frozen berries
250 ml (1 c) good beef stock
20 ml (4 t) brown sugar
25 ml (5 t) cherry brandy
50 ml dry red wine
salt and freshly ground black pepper
lemon juice

Preheat the oven to 220 °C (425 °F). Season the fillet with salt and pepper, and sprinkle with the flour. Dip it in the milk and then in the nuts, pressing the nuts firmly onto the meat. Heat the butter and oil in a pan with an ovenproof handle. Add the thyme. Fry the fillet until golden brown on the outside. Place the pan with the meat in the oven and oven-roast until just done. Remove from the oven and transfer the meat to a serving plate.

Return the pan to the stove and add the berries, stock and brown sugar. Heat slowly until the sugar has melted and boil until the sauce turns syrupy. Add the cherry brandy and red wine, and reduce once more until syrupy. Season with salt and pepper and a generous dash of lemon juice. Slice the fillet and pour the sauce on top. Serve with oven-grilled fresh pineapple and braised tomato sauce (p. 76).

Serves 2.

Orange River mud pudding with wild berries

We were pleased to discover the recipe for this deliciously moist dessert comes from *You*. Niel says it's a hit with his patrons.

250 g butter

15 ml (1 T) whisky or brandy

180 ml (¾ c) sugar

250 g dark chocolate,
   finely chopped

375 ml (1½ c) hot water

375 ml (1½ c) self-raising flour

60 ml (¼ c) cocoa

2 extra-large eggs

5 ml (1 t) vanilla essence

Preheat the oven to 180 °C (350 °F). Spray a medium-sized ovenproof dish with nonstick spray.

Slowly melt the butter in a saucepan. Add the whisky, sugar, chopped chocolate and water, stirring until the chocolate has just melted and the mixture is smooth.

Sift the self-raising flour and cocoa together and gently beat into the chocolate mixture. Add the eggs and vanilla essence and beat until just blended. Turn the batter into the prepared dish and bake for 40-45 minutes or until a skewer comes out clean when inserted into the centre of the pudding. Serve lukewarm or cold with a variety of berries and cream, if preferred.

Makes a medium-sized pudding.

At the Duineveld High School's hotel school Susina Jooste teaches the children to prepare real food, attractively. These days Lizbé Jonas, who was my assistant in You's test kitchen for many years, also shows them how things are done.

And the children rose to the occasion. During the festival they ran their own restaurant on the banks of the Orange River. Festival-goers could drop in at any time, early to late, for some of the famous biltong soup and nutty sweet potato caramel tart, laid out on long, white-clothed tables standing in the shade of trees and umbrellas.

Susina says their food is inspired by local ingredients: dates, sultanas, brinjals and spinach, pecan nuts and biltong, lentils and game; and they want to tell visitors more about the Kalahari, through their food.

Biltong soup

Niel Stemmet of Le Must served this soup at his restaurant some fifteen years ago. Since then there have been many improvisations. The school's version is less rich than the original.

125 ml (½ c) butter

2 beef stock cubes

10 ml (2 t) coarsely ground black pepper

2 ml (½ t) freshly grated nutmeg

2 ml (½ t) freshly ground coriander

250 ml (1 c) cake flour

500 ml (2 c) milk

1,5 litres (6 c) boiling water

250 ml (1 c) coarsely grated Cheddar cheese

200 g finely sliced moist biltong

cream and port

100 g blue cheese, grated

bread sticks for serving

Melt the butter in a heavy-based saucepan. Crumble the stock cubes and add along with the spices. Add the flour and heat, stirring continuously until the flour begins to simmer. Mix the milk and boiling water, and slowly stir into the flour mixture. Stirring continuously, heat over medium heat until the mixture begins to simmer and thicken.

Remove from the heat and stir in the Cheddar cheese and half the biltong. Do not allow the mixture to boil again. Keep warm until ready to serve. Stir in a little cream and port just before serving if desired.

Ladle the hot soup into deep soup bowls and scatter a little of the remaining biltong and the blue cheese on top. Serve with bread sticks.

Serves 8-10.

Spinach pie

Well-known cookery book author Mariëtte Crafford demonstrated this dish, made with ingredients grown in the Kalahari, at Duineveld High School's food-and-wine festival.

WHOLE-WHEAT SHORT-CRUST PASTRY

250 ml (1 c) whole-wheat flour

500 ml (2 c) cake flour

250 ml (1 c) cornflour

pinch salt

360 g cold butter

2,5 ml (½ t) cream of tartar

100 ml ice-cold water

1 egg white, lightly whisked

1 egg yolk, lightly whisked and mixed
　with milk

SPINACH FILLING

300-500 g fresh spinach leaves, well rinsed,
　ribs removed and cut into 2-cm strips

ground sea salt

60 ml (¼ c) olive oil

handful basil leaves, shredded,
　or 15 ml (1 T) dried basil

2 eggs

250 g feta cheese, coarsely crumbled,
　or cottage cheese

60-125 ml (¼ -½ c) sultanas, soaked in boiling
　water for 15 minutes

salt and freshly ground black pepper to taste

Combine the whole-wheat flour, cake flour, cornflour and salt. Grate in the butter and rub in until the mixture is crumbly. Dissolve the cream of tartar in the ice-cold water and add just enough of the liquid to the flour mixture to make a pastry that is easy to roll out. Divide the pastry into two pieces, one slightly bigger than the other. Press into flat circles, wrap in plastic wrap and chill for at least 15 minutes or until needed. Remove the pastry from the fridge at least 15 minutes before rolling out.

On a floured surface, roll out the larger piece of pastry until thin. Grease a 28-cm springform cake tin and line the base and sides with the pastry. Trim the edges with a sharp, unserrated knife. Prick the base of the crust and chill. Roll out the other piece of pastry and cut out a circle the size of the tin. Cover with plastic wrap and set aside.

Preheat the oven to 180 °C (350 °F).

Place the spinach in a large mixing bowl and add a generous amount of sea salt. Mix well and allow to stand for 1 hour. Rinse well and pat dry with paper towelling. Slightly heat the olive oil in a pan and add half the spinach. Sauté gently until the leaves begin to wilt. Remove to a side dish and repeat with the rest of the spinach. Add to the spinach in the dish and add the basil.

Beat the eggs, add the cheese and mix well. Drain the sultanas and add. Mix with the spinach mixture and season with salt and pepper.

Brush the unbaked crust with beaten egg white and spoon the filling into the crust, spreading evenly. Place the pastry circle on top and fold the edges over the sides. Brush with beaten egg yolk and milk and bake for 20-30 minutes until the crust is golden brown and done. Allow to cool slightly before removing the pan from the oven. Cut into slices with a sharp knife. Serve lukewarm.

Makes a medium-sized pie.

Chakalaka muffins

"We unexpectedly had to make a plate of eats one morning," says Susina. "Ida, one of our kitchen staff, suggested we spoon a little chakalaka on top of each muffin so we wouldn't still have to think of a spread. Everyone loved the muffins and now they're served regularly with morning coffee at the school."

500 ml (2 c) cake flour
10 ml (2 t) baking powder
pinch salt
5 ml (1 t) garlic-and-herb mixture
  (preferably Ina Paarman's)
1 extra-large egg
100 ml sunflower oil
200 ml milk or water
200 ml chakalaka
100 g (250 ml) grated Cheddar cheese

Preheat the oven to 180 °C (350 °F). Grease the hollows of a muffin pan well with margarine or spray with nonstick spray.

Sift all the dry ingredients together. Mix the egg, oil and milk or water together and mix lightly with the flour mixture. Spoon a large tablespoonful of the batter into each hollow of the muffin pan. Spoon a tablespoonful of chakalaka on top of the batter and sprinkle with grated cheese. Bake for about 20 minutes or until the muffins are done.

Serve hot – because these muffins are so deliciously moist and flavoursome they can be served as is.

Makes about 12 muffins.

Nutty sweet potato caramel tart

Former women's magazine editor and food fundi René Barnard lived for some time in Upington, where she developed this recipe. At Duineveld High they serve the tart topped with spun sugar. They've perfected the art and gave a demonstration during the festival.

CRUST

300 g frozen puff pastry, thawed and rolled out until thinner

FILLING

150 g (1½ packets) pecan nuts, chopped

60 g butter

60 g soft brown sugar

pinch salt

3 eggs

190 ml honey

5 ml (1 t) ground ginger

500 ml (2 c) cooked sweet potatoes, diced

Preheat the oven to 190 °C (375 °F). Grease a 24-cm pie dish with butter or margarine or spray with nonstick spray. Line the dish with puff pastry.

Sprinkle 125 ml (½ c) of the nuts over the base of the crust. Cream the butter and sugar. Add the salt, eggs, honey and ginger, and mix well. Spoon the diced sweet potato into the crust and pour over the egg mixture. Sprinkle the rest of the nuts on top and bake for about 45 minutes or until done.

Serve lukewarm.

Makes a medium-sized tart.

Groenvallei Nursery is a green oasis in the town. Dirkie Visser has a way with plants – he learnt from his father who, from early on, taught the children where to find succulents in the veld. Before there were cafés on the streets of Upington, they started a tea garden in the nursery where people could enjoy tea and cake among the flowers and trees, in peaceful surroundings. His sister, Beate Strydom, does the baking nowadays.

Strawberry cheesecake

This cheesecake is ridiculously easy to make. It contains no eggs and will still be slightly soft after the baking time, but firms when chilled.

CRUST

125 g butter

1 packet (200 g) Tennis biscuits, crushed

FILLING

2 tins (397 g each) condensed milk

2 containers (250 g each) cream cheese or smooth cottage cheese, strained through a muslin cloth if very fresh

125 ml (½ c) lemon juice

fresh strawberries for decoration (optional)

Preheat the oven to 180 °C (350 °F). Melt the butter and stir in the crushed biscuits. Press the mixture into the base of a 20-cm loose-bottomed cake tin.

To make the filling, beat all the ingredients together and pour onto the crust. Bake for 15 minutes. Allow to cool completely before removing from the pan. Chill in the fridge before decorating with fresh strawberry slices, if preferred.

Serve with cream.

Makes a medium-sized cheesecake.

Namibian **choice**

Namibians are genial people who enjoy their food. They meet in coffee shops and street cafés, and quench their thirst with a quick Tafel at one of Windhoek's colourful beer gardens. The influence of German food culture is apparent everywhere, and everyone enjoys *belegten Brötchens* (sandwiches with fillings), *Eisbein* (pork shank) with *Kartoffeln* (potatoes) and *Sauerkraut*. There's no shortage of venison dishes either, prepared well at restaurants and especially at safari lodges. We've also been privileged to taste the giant wild mushroom, omajova, which appears on termite heaps after the rains.

I have always loved Namibia and will grasp at any opportunity to get there. As luck would have it, we unexpectedly found ourselves in Windhoek for the city's first arts festival at the end of February 2000.

It's a clean city, and everywhere you see people relaxing in streets and parks. There are a number of castles, all fine examples of German influence on the architecture. The sunsets are indescribably beautiful – even more so if you view them from the top of a hill, surrounded by open grassy plains, camel-thorn trees and sheltering wild animals.

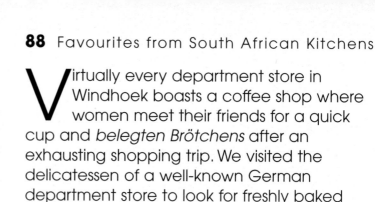

Virtually every department store in Windhoek boasts a coffee shop where women meet their friends for a quick cup and *belegten Brötchens* after an exhausting shopping trip. We visited the delicatessen of a well-known German department store to look for freshly baked goodies such as *Bretzels* and rye bread to enjoy with real German cold meats, for a picnic: *Knackwurst* and *Kasegriller*, *Rauchfleisch* (thinly sliced smoked fillet, rather like biltong) and *Kabanossi*, a mature garlic salami which resembles thin dried sausage.

Windhoek also has a street café culture, with people meeting for light meals and, of course, a beer. The Craft Café in the Namibian Craft Centre is unique – meals are served in rustic pottery, the coffee mugs have grotesque shapes and recycled glasses are used for milk shakes and health drinks.

For the full Namibian experience, however, you have to visit a beer garden or some of the traditional German restaurants. Joe's Beer House is *the* meeting place in Windhoek. At night it is packed with people turning up for a draught beer and *Eisbein*. At the Windhoek Brauhaus you'll experience true German hospitality and enjoy traditional foods. People who wish to dine in style book a table at Gathemann's Restaurant, where venison dishes and specialities such as Lüderitz oysters and fresh asparagus from Swakopmund are beautifully served.

But the highlight of a visit to Namibia is a bush safari. Whether you stay in luxurious colonial style at Hunters Namibia Safaris, just outside Windhoek, or in an old German stone homestead in the south, beside the Noachabeb, it remains an unforgettable experience to take an early-morning ride in a Land Rover, drink coffee from a flask at a water hole while watching kudu and giraffe, and to sit at a table laid with silver and crystal, enjoying a meal out of Africa . . .

The Stegmann family run the Craft Café in the Craft Centre. Mathilde, a potter, makes all the rustic ware in which the food is served, and her daughter, Heike, does the cooking. The menu is a model of fresh, wholesome food. They enjoy creative cooking; all the food is home-made, everything they use they made themselves, and the ingredients come from their farm. The initial aim was to capture the tourist market, but the Craft Café has become a popular venue for the inhabitants of Windhoek as well.

Decadent chocolate cake

This cake is made with real chocolate and has a chocolate and cream cheese filling.

CAKE

200 g butter

180 ml (¾ c) golden syrup

100 g dark chocolate

60 ml (¼ c) cocoa

250 ml (1 c) white sugar

200 ml buttermilk

2 extra-large eggs

500 ml (2 c) cake flour

7 ml (1½ t) bicarbonate of soda

FILLING

125 ml (½ c) strong black coffee

2 extra-large egg yolks

60 ml (¼ c) white sugar

100 g dark chocolate, finely chopped

250 g (1 container) mascarpone
   or cream cheese

30 ml (2 T) brandy

cocoa for decoration

Preheat the oven to 160 °C (325 °F). Grease two 20-cm cake tins well with butter or margarine or spray with nonstick spray. Line with baking paper.

Place the butter, syrup, chocolate, cocoa, sugar and half the buttermilk in a saucepan and heat slowly until melted, but do not bring to the boil. Beat the eggs and remaining buttermilk together.

Sift the flour and bicarbonate of soda in a mixing bowl. Stirring continuously, add the egg and buttermilk mixture slowly to the dry ingredients, followed by the hot cocoa mixture.

Spoon the batter into the prepared tins and bake for 35-40 minutes until done or a skewer comes out clean when inserted into the centre of the cake. Cool the cakes in the tins before turning out onto a wire rack to cool completely. (The cakes are very moist and do not rise much.)

Carefully halve each cake layer horizontally and sprinkle the prepared coffee over each of the four layers.

Beat the egg yolks and sugar in a glass bowl over hot water until thick and light. Remove from the heat. Beat the chocolate, mascarpone or cream cheese and brandy into the sugar mixture, beating until the mixture is stiff. Place one of the cake layers in a 20-cm loose-bottomed tin lined with baking paper. Spread a third of the filling over the cake layer and place another cake layer on top. Repeat with the remaining filling and cake layers, ending with a cake layer. Place in the fridge for at least 2-3 hours to set. Remove the cake tin ring, transfer the cake to a serving platter and dust the top with cocoa. Serve with coffee.

Makes a large cake.

Goulash

At the Windhoek Brauhaus, goulash is served in a hollowed-out rye loaf.

5 rashers bacon, chopped

1,4 kg stewing beef, cubed

4 medium onions, finely chopped

6 cloves garlic, finely chopped

30 ml (2 T) oil

45 ml (3 T) paprika

7 ml (1½ t) cumin seeds

80 ml (⅓ c) cake flour

60 ml (¼ c) red wine vinegar

60 ml (¼ c) tomato paste

750 ml (3 c) beef stock

250 ml (1 c) water

125 ml (½ c) beer

7 ml (1½ t) salt

3 ml (generous ½ t) coarsely ground black pepper

2 red sweet peppers, seeded and finely chopped

2 bay leaves

4 large potatoes, peeled and diced

chopped chives

In a large saucepan, fry the bacon until crisp and remove from the pan. Brown the beef cubes in the pan fat and remove from the pan. Reduce the heat and fry the onions and garlic in the oil until golden brown. Stir in the paprika, cumin seeds and cake flour and simmer for about 2 minutes.

Mix in the vinegar and tomato paste and simmer for 1 minute, beating continuously. Stir in the stock, water and beer. Season with salt and pepper and also add the sweet peppers, bay leaves, bacon and meat. Bring to the boil while stirring continuously. Simmer, uncovered, for about 45 minutes, stirring occasionally.

Add the potatoes and simmer for another 30 minutes, uncovered, until the potatoes are tender. Season with extra salt and pepper to taste. Garnish with freshly chopped chives.

Serves 6.

Gathemann's Restaurant offers an eye-catching selection of German continental baked delights such as apple strudel, plum tart, pecan nut tart, pear cake and cherry cake. The cooking skills of the owner and chef, Urs Gamma, display more than a touch of Austrian perfectionism. In Namibia, fresh ingredients are always hard to come by, so when they're lucky enough to find a large supply they use as many fresh as possible and preserve the rest. While we were taking photographs, Urs was cooking fresh plums to make a sauce he could store for later use.

Apple strudel

Making strudel dough is quite an art, so we used phyllo pastry instead.

4 sheets phyllo pastry
melted butter

FILLING
1 kg Granny Smith apples, peeled,
   cored and thinly sliced
125 ml (½ c) seedless raisins
125 ml (½ c) soft brown sugar
80 ml (⅓ c) walnuts, chopped
5 ml (1 t) cinnamon
finely grated rind of 1 lemon

Preheat the oven to 200 °C (400 °F). Grease a large baking sheet with butter or margarine or spray with nonstick spray. Spread each sheet of phyllo pastry with melted butter and arrange on top of each other. Spread the top layer with melted butter and sprinkle the apples, raisins, sugar, walnuts, cinnamon and lemon rind on top. Roll up and place on the prepared baking sheet. Bake for about 15-20 minutes until crisp and pale brown and heated through.

Serve lukewarm with cream, if desired.

Makes a medium-sized roll.

Plum tart

Any fruit, such as sliced pears or apples, can be used instead of the plums.

PASTRY
1 extra-large egg
150 ml icing sugar, sifted
1 ml (¼ t) salt
125 ml (½ c) toasted hazelnuts, ground
125 g butter
375 ml (1½ c) cake flour, sifted
15 ml (1 T) milk

FILLING
15-20 ripe plums, halved and stoned
30 ml (2 T) brown sugar
125 ml (½ c) cream
1 egg, whisked

Preheat the oven to 200 °C (400 °F) and grease a 22-cm pie dish with butter or margarine or spray with nonstick spray. Line with baking paper.

Beat the egg, icing sugar and salt together well. Add the ground hazelnuts and butter, beating until thick, light and creamy. Sift over the flour and mix until crumbly. Gather the crumbs together – if the mixture is too dry to form a ball, add a little milk. Knead lightly into a ball and cover with plastic wrap. Chill for at least 30 minutes.

Roll out the pastry on a floured surface and cut into a circle the size of the pie dish. Place in the pie dish. Cut out a circle of baking paper large enough to cover the pastry circle and place on top. Sprinkle dried beans on the baking paper and bake the pastry for about 10 minutes until the edges start to turn brown. Remove from the oven and remove the beans and baking paper.

Slice the plums and arrange in concentric circles on the pie crust. Sprinkle with brown sugar and bake for 15 minutes at 200 °C (400 °F). Meanwhile, beat the cream and egg together.

Reduce the heat to 180 °C (350 °F), pour the cream mixture over the plums and bake for another 10-15 minutes or until set.

Makes a large tart.

Her Bushman menu and typically Namibian fare made Kim Vosloo of the Kleines Heim guesthouse a winner in the Namibian holiday and travel expo competition. One evening, she prepared the winning menu specially for us, so we could taste the omajova, or giant mushrooms, which grow on termite heaps after the rains, and must be picked at sunrise. She turned the mushrooms into a delicious soup and served it in ostrich egg shells.

Omajova soup

Omajova is the Herero name for giant mushrooms. We used button mushrooms instead.

1 large omajova, stem included,
   or about 750 g button mushrooms
1 large onion, chopped
15 ml (1 T) olive oil
250 ml (1 c) dry white wine
500 ml (2 c) vegetable stock
250 ml (1 c) cream
5 ml (1 t) salt
freshly ground black pepper to taste
a few fresh coriander leaves,
   chopped (dhania)
grated rind of 1 lemon

Slice the mushrooms and sauté with the onion in the olive oil until tender. Add the white wine and stock and simmer. Add the cream and salt and bring to the boil. Remove from the heat and season with freshly ground black pepper. Heat just before serving and stir in the fresh coriander leaves and lemon rind.

Serve hot.
Serves 3.

Hunters Namibia Safaris, Marina and Joof Lampbrecht's world-class hunting farm where foreign trophy hunters come for a classic hunting safari, is about an hour's drive from Windhoek. At the entrance, visitors are greeted by the Namibian flag and their own national flags. The South African flag was hoisted for us.

The double-track road takes you across grassy plains to the imposing main homestead, built of stone and with a neat thatched roof. The interior is colonial – dark mahogany and leather furniture, real linen, hand-embroidered bed linen, imported silver and large fireplaces decorated with African art. Joof and Marina love the area in which they live and work, and enjoy entertaining their international guests stylishly. At night the homestead is lit by lanterns along the footpaths.

We chatted until late around the dining table, warmed by the fire crackling in the fireplace. The dining table was laid with silver and crystal and we were treated to mouthwatering dishes, a combination of local and German cuisine.

Although Marina has had no formal cookery training, she enjoys experimenting with food and makes extensive use of fruit and toasted seeds and nuts with venison dishes.

Waldorf salad

This is Marina's version of the well-known salad.

125 ml (½ c) mayonnaise

45 ml (3 T) sour cream

30 ml (2 T) fresh lemon juice

3 ml (generous ½ t) curry powder

5 ml (1 t) white sugar

4 Granny Smith apples, cored
   and cut into wedges

375 ml (1½ c) celery stalks, chopped

200 g (2 packets) walnuts, coarsely chopped

Italian parsley

Blend the mayonnaise, sour cream, lemon juice, curry powder and sugar together and set aside. Lightly mix the apple wedges, celery and walnuts. Moisten with the dressing and sprinkle with parsley.
   Serves 4-6.

Smoked venison salad

1 smoked loin of venison or fairly moist
   game biltong, thinly sliced

1 packet mixed lettuce leaves

100 ml toasted pine nuts or sunflower seeds

125 ml (½ c) olive oil

50 ml balsamic vinegar

15 ml (1 T) lemon juice

1 ml (¼ t) salt

freshly ground black pepper

Arrange the meat slices on the lettuce leaves and scatter the pine nuts on top. Blend the olive oil, balsamic vinegar and lemon juice. Season with salt and freshly ground black pepper and sprinkle over the salad.
   Serves 4-6.

Smoked venison salad

Whole roast venison fillet

The quantities in this recipe are for a gemsbok fillet and will vary depending on the type of fillet used – reduce the ingredients for a springbok fillet for instance, and increase them for a zebra or eland fillet.

15 ml (1 T) soy sauce

1 whole venison fillet, such as gemsbok

45 ml (3 T) Dijon mustard

5 ml (1 t) oil

whole black peppercorns, crushed

salt

Rub the soy sauce into the fillet. Mix the mustard and oil and spread over the entire fillet. Roll in the coarse pepper and leave to rest in the fridge for at least 1 hour. Season lightly with salt just before roasting. Roast over medium coals until medium-done. Rest for 5 minutes before carving.

Serve with fruit sauces such as curried apricot cream or mustard and mango sauce.

Serves 8.

Curried apricot cream

100 g soft dried apricots, chopped

hot water

generous tot brandy

80 ml (⅓ c) sour cream

100 ml mayonnaise

3 ml (generous ½ t) curry powder

salt and freshly ground black pepper to taste

Soak the apricots overnight in hot water to which brandy has been added. Mix the remaining ingredients well. Drain the apricots and fold into the sour-cream mixture.

Makes 200 ml.

Mustard and mango sauce

2 ripe mangoes, skinned and diced

22 ml (1½ T) yellow or black mustard seeds

1 ripe banana, chopped

30 ml (2 T) finely grated fresh ginger

2 cloves garlic, crushed

125 ml (½ c) grapefruit juice

10 ml (2 t) sherry vinegar

7 ml (1½ t) chilli oil

15 ml (1 T) honey

salt and freshly ground black pepper to taste

Reserve a quarter of the diced mango. Place all the ingredients in a food processor and process until smooth. Fold in the reserved diced mango. The sauce keeps well in the fridge for three days.

Makes 250 ml (1 c).

Phyllo tower with cream and fruit

6 sheets phyllo pastry

100 ml melted butter

FILLING

180 ml (¾ c) thick cream

80 ml (⅓ c) icing sugar, sifted

180 ml (¾ c) thick plain yoghurt

2 ml (½ 5) almond essence

6 ripe nectarines (or other fresh fruit or berries)

icing sugar

fresh mint leaves for decoration

Preheat the oven to 180 °C (350 °F). Cut the pastry into fairly large equal squares, about 4 cm x 4 cm each.

Lightly grease two baking sheets with melted butter and place a few phyllo pastry squares on each baking sheet. Brush lightly with melted butter and cover each with another square. Do not brush the top layer of pastry with butter. Repeat with the remaining phyllo pastry. Bake for 4-5 minutes or until crisp and dry but still pale in colour – do not overbake the pastry.

Whip the cream and icing sugar together until stiff. Carefully fold in the yoghurt and almond essence. Chill until just before assembling the dessert.

Slice the nectarines. Assemble the dessert just before serving. Use separate plates and place one double layer of phyllo pastry on each plate. Top with yoghurt cream and a few thin nectarine slices, and cover with another double layer of phyllo pastry. Top with another scoop of yoghurt cream and nectarine slices. Dust with icing sugar and decorate with fresh mint leaves and nectarine slices.

Serve immediately.

Serves 4-6.

Not far from Grünau in southern Namibia, lies Noachabeb, like a green oasis among the rocky hills of the Karasberg. At one time it was a halfway house for German soldiers. The house was built of stone, and the former dining hall, kitchen and infirmary have been replaced by a stylish homestead, complete with turret. Erich and Zelda von Schauroth have been farming here for some time. At Noachabeb – a Nama word meaning "flat, shiny stones" – there are mainly springbok and kudu. Previously, foreign hunters were allowed to hunt here on request, but Erich and Zelda soon decided to do the hunting themselves.

As they're close to the highway, they opened a biltong stall, the first in southern Namibia. Apart from biltong and dried sausage they also sell stuffed leg, rolled ribs, shoulder and fillet medallions.

Zelda has always been interested in cooking and attends courses and demonstrations whenever she can. Since they started offering guest rooms, they've been doing lots of entertaining. They have many foreign visitors, mainly because of Erich's contact with his German family. Zelda serves their guests traditional fare, naturally including venison.

Biltong spread

At Noachabeb this spread is served with whole-wheat bread or biscuits.

1 medium onion, chopped

250 g mushrooms

15 ml (1 T) oil

150 g finely grated biltong

150 ml mayonnaise

250 g smooth cottage cheese

Sauté the onion and mushrooms in heated oil until tender and done. Cool and chop finely. Add the remaining ingredients and process until smooth.

Makes 750 ml (3 c).

Zelda likes to serve sweet accompaniments with venison – pumpkin fritters, sweet potatoes or carrots and bottled quinces – and, of course, roast potatoes.

Leg of venison with red wine sauce

Leg of venison stuffed with bacon and served with a red wine sauce.

buttermilk

1 leg of springbok, about 2-2,5 kg

3 cloves garlic, peeled and
  cut into slivers (optional)

125-250 g bacon pieces

dried rosemary

salt and freshly ground black pepper

250 ml (1 c) red wine

GRAVY

50 ml port

30 ml (2 T) cake flour

15 ml (1 T) sugar or apricot jam

60 ml (¼ c) cream

Pour just enough buttermilk over the meat to cover. Marinate for 1-2 days.

Preheat the oven to 160 °C (325 °F). Pat the leg dry. Using a sharp knife, make small incisions all over the leg and stuff with slivers of garlic and bacon pieces.

Place the leg in a casserole dish and sprinkle with rosemary and black pepper, and a little salt. Pour over the red wine, cover and bake for about 2-2½ hours or until the leg is done, but not dry. Remove the covering and place under the grill until golden brown. Transfer the leg to a serving platter and leave to rest in the warming drawer to make carving easier.

Add enough boiling water to the pan juices to make up 500 ml (2 c) and bring to the boil. Add the port. Thicken the gravy with cake flour mixed with a little water. Season with sugar or jam and salt and pepper to taste. Stir in the cream and serve the gravy separately with the carved meat.

Serves 6-8.

A selection of roast venison, served with roast potatoes, pumpkin fritters, bottled quinces and other vegetables

Rolled springbok rib with dried peaches

Rolled rib stuffed with dried peaches.

1 springbok rib, boned
buttermilk
dried peaches, soaked in
   sweet wine
salt and pepper
125 ml (½ c) sweet wine
125 ml (½ c) red wine
125 ml (½ c) meat stock
1 bay leaf
15 ml (1 T) cake flour
15 ml (1 T) cream

Marinate the rib for 1-2 days in buttermilk.

Preheat the oven to 160 °C (325 °F). Unroll the rib and arrange the dried peaches on top. Roll up again and secure with string. Season with salt and pepper to taste and place in a casserole dish.

Add the sweet and red wines, stock and bay leaf. Cover and bake for about 1½-2 hours or until the rib is cooked but not dry. Remove the covering and grill until golden brown. Place on a serving platter and leave to rest in the warming drawer.

Add enough boiling water to the pan juices to make up 250 ml (1 c). Thicken with cake flour mixed with a little water and bring to the boil. Add cream and serve with the sliced rib.

Serves 4-6.

Boned shoulder of springbok with mustard and white wine sauce

Bacon and mustard impart a special flavour to this shoulder of springbok.

1 shoulder of springbok, boned
buttermilk
prepared mustard
125 g bacon
salt and freshly ground black
   pepper to taste
125 ml (½ c) dry white wine
125 ml (½ c) meat stock
rind and juice of 1 lemon
a sprig of parsley
30 ml (2 T) cake flour
15 ml (1 T) cream

Marinate the meat for 2-3 days in buttermilk.

Preheat the oven to 160 °C (325 °F). Pat the meat dry and open out flat on a working surface. Spread the meaty side with prepared mustard such as Dijon and arrange the rashers of bacon on top. Roll up and secure with string. Layer remaining bacon on top and season with salt and freshly ground black pepper. Place in a casserole dish.

Add the wine, meat stock, lemon rind and juice and parsley. Cover and bake for about 2-2½ hours until done but not dry. Remove the covering and grill until golden brown. Transfer to a serving platter and leave to rest in the warming drawer.

Add boiling water to the pan juices to make up 500 ml (2 c). Thicken with flour mixed with a little water and bring to the boil. Stir in the cream and serve with the carved meat.

Serves 6-8.

Vanilla chocolate pudding

Easy to make and a delectable conclusion to any meal.

1 tin (397 g) condensed milk
250 ml (1 c) cream, whipped
1 packet instant vanilla pudding
1 packet instant chocolate
   pudding
1 packet finger biscuits
1 tin (410 g) youngberries
cornflour

Divide the condensed milk and cream between two mixing bowls. Add a condensed milk can of water to each bowl. Add a packet of instant pudding to each bowl and beat until well blended.

Arrange a layer of biscuits in a fairly small oblong dish. Spoon the chocolate mixture on top. Arrange another layer of biscuits on top and spoon the vanilla mixture on top. Chill until set.

Drain the youngberries, but reserve the syrup. Boil the syrup with about 10-15 ml (2-3 t) cornflour to thicken the sauce. Add the youngberries and mix.

Cut the pudding into pieces. Serve with the youngberry sauce.

Serves 4-6.

Vanilla chocolate pudding

Nutty meringue

Zelda serves this meringue with after-dinner coffee.

whites of 3 extra-large eggs
250 ml (1 c) castor sugar
pinch cream of tartar
1 packet (200 g) Tennis biscuits, coarsely broken
1 packet (100 g) nuts, such as pecan nuts, chopped
500 ml (2 c) cream, chilled
125 ml (½ c) icing sugar
whole green fig preserve

Preheat the oven to 180 °C (350 °F). Line a baking sheet with a sheet of baking paper and dust with cornflour.

Beat the egg whites until foamy. Add the sugar, a little at a time, and beat with the cream of tartar until stiff and glossy. Fold in the biscuits and nuts.

Shape the mixture into a round on the baking paper and bake for 25 minutes.

Cool and store in an airtight container until needed.

Whip the cream and icing sugar together until stiff and drop dollops of the mixture on top of the meringue. Decorate with slices of green figs.

Makes a medium-sized tart.

Fillet medallions with a creamy mushroom sauce

Erich's favourite, which they serve with rice.

2 medium onions, sliced
250 g mushrooms, sliced
250 g bacon, chopped
oil
generous tot of sherry
125 ml (½ c) chutney
250 ml (1 c) cream
1 springbok fillet, cut into medallions
salt and freshly ground black pepper to taste

Fry the onions, mushrooms and bacon in heated oil until nicely browned and done. Add the sherry, chutney and cream and bring to the boil. Simmer for a few minutes.

Season the medallions to taste with salt and pepper and fry in heated oil until just done. Serve with the mushroom sauce.

Serves 4.

Fillet medallions with a ceamy mushroom sauce

Boland **bounty**

The winelands of the Boland offer breathtaking vistas of undulating, vine-covered mountain slopes and stately Cape Dutch homes with thatched roofs and whitewashed walls, nestling under ancient oak trees. Many date back to the 1600's, when Governor Simon van der Stel granted land to the first pioneers.

The wine farms in the Stellenbosch and Paarl districts are world-famous – no longer for their choice wines only, but also for the wonderful variety of authentic Cape foods served with them. There are several world-class restaurants in the area, and you can also picnic on the banks of the Eerste River or visit an excellent cookery school. You can go to offal evenings and experience the authentic Boland flavour of waterblommetjie bredie (stew), or sample a variety of jams made from the abundant produce of the orchards on a centuries-old fruit farm. And honest Cape country cooking is enjoyed on enormous stoeps, under pergolas covered in vines.

There are several restaurants to try on the well-known Spier wine estate outside Stellenbosch, and you can also enjoy a leisurely picnic on the banks of the Eerste River. Best of all, you can buy all the picnic food at the farm stall on the estate, then relax in the cool shade of the trees.

Seidelberg, another centuries-old wine estate, on the far side of Paarl, hosts special offal evenings, serving delicacies such as baked sheep's heads. Here, among the vineyards, Hetta van der Merwe enjoys treating guests to this old, nearly forgotten, speciality. Porcupine quills and guinea fowl feathers in clay pots, and the occasional antelope horn introduce a hint of the Karoo to the Boland mountains.

There are several top-class fruit farms in the area. At Riverside, near Simondium, the most delicious jams are made from plums, nectarines, grapes ... and fresh farm bread with fresh fruit constitutes an entire meal. Fresh fruit is used in mustard and curry sauces to impart flavour to a leg of mutton, chicken and even venison.

The Spier estate is also home to a top-class cookery school, The Institute of Culinary Arts, which is also recognised overseas. But this was not where we met its enthusiastic owner, Laetitia Prinsloo, for the first time; we met at her home, high on the slopes of the Jonkers-hoek Mountains. Standing on the balcony late one afternoon, I could see the mountain turning pink in the twilight. In 1998, when I asked her to cook a Christmas meal for us, she decided, after much thought, on a pink Christmas – as pink as her beloved mountain and using ingredients indigenous to the area: lots of fruit served with ham and duck, an ice-cold pink strawberry soup and pink sparkling wine, served with a tumbling nectarine.

The old workers' quarters on the Spier estate outside Stellenbosch have been converted into a farm stall selling all sorts of home-made products: jams, preserves, pickles and sauces. At the deli counter you can buy freshly baked bread, as well as cheeses, spreads and cold meats, and choose from an array of salads for your picnic basket. Add a bottle of wine and cake for dessert, and you're all set to relax in the shade and watch the children feeding crumbs to ducks on the pond.

Gherkin and olive salad

500 g gherkins, thickly sliced

4 stalks celery, sliced into thin rings

250 g stoned olives

1 onion, sliced

50 ml olive oil

Mix all the ingredients and spoon into a salad bowl.
Serves 4-6.

Fruit kebabs

Cut fruit in season such as pineapple, melon, watermelon, kiwi fruit, apples, pears and peaches into large chunks and thread onto skewers.

Rosemary potato salad

SALAD DRESSING

250 ml (1 c) mayonnaise

125 ml (½ c) fresh cream

30 ml (2 T) prepared mustard

salt and freshly ground black pepper to taste

SALAD

1 kg baby potatoes, scrubbed and boiled
   until tender

3 hard-boiled eggs, cut into wedges

a few sprigs fresh rosemary

Blend all the ingredients for the salad dressing and pour over the potatoes. Add the eggs and rosemary and mix lightly.
   Serves 6-8.

Mushroom salad

125 ml (½ c) wine vinegar

150 ml olive oil

45 ml (3 T) sugar

2 ml (½ t) salt

1 clove garlic, crushed

a few freshly chopped herbs such as thyme,
   basil and marjoram

750 g button mushrooms, wiped clean with a
   damp cloth

5 ml (1 t) lemon juice

30 ml (2 T) olive oil

Place all the ingredients except the mushrooms, lemon juice and 30 ml (2 T) olive oil in a saucepan and bring to the boil. Switch off the stove immediately and add the mushrooms. Leave on the hot plate for 5 minutes. Spoon a little of the sauce in the salad bowl and place the mushrooms on top. Blend the lemon juice and olive oil and pour on top.
   Serves 8.

Tomato and cheese salad

SALAD DRESSING

125 ml (½ c) olive oil

60 ml (¼ c) water

60 ml (¼ c) white wine vinegar

20 ml (4 t) mixed dried herbs

10 ml (2 t) sugar

SALAD

500 g mozzarella cheese, thinly sliced

5-6 tomatoes, thinly sliced

a few basil leaves

Blend all the ingredients for the salad dressing and chill until needed.
   Arrange alternating layers of the cheese and tomato slices on a salad platter, moisten with the dressing and garnish with a few basil leaves.
   Serves 6.

Roast vegetable salad

2 medium brinjals, cut into fairly thick slices

salt

10 courgettes, sliced

1 large red sweet pepper, seeded and sliced
   into strips

1 large yellow sweet pepper, seeded
   and sliced into strips

250 g button mushrooms

175 g baby corn

175 g young green beans

250 g cherry tomatoes

15 whole cloves garlic, cleaned

milk

oil

1-2 medium onions, sliced into rings

cake flour

whisked egg

fresh basil leaves (optional)

lemon juice

salt and freshly ground black pepper

olive oil and balsamic vinegar

Sprinkle the brinjal slices with salt and leave for about 10 minutes. Rinse and pat dry with paper towelling. Arrange all the vegetables, except the garlic and onions on baking sheets. Arrange the tomatoes on a separate baking sheet.

Grill under the oven grill until pale brown. Turn frequently. Place the cloves of garlic in a saucepan, add a little milk and boil for 1 minute. Drain and fry the garlic in oil until brown.

Blanch the onion rings in boiling water until tender but still crisp. Drain and roll in flour, then in egg and in the flour again. Fry in fairly deep oil until brown. Arrange all the vegetables on a fairly large serving platter, garnish with fresh basil if preferred and season with a little lemon juice and salt and pepper to taste.

Serve with a sprinkling of olive oil and balsamic vinegar.

Serves 10.

Pasta salad

SALAD DRESSING

125 ml (½ c) olive oil

60 ml (¼ c) white wine vinegar

5 ml (1 t) lemon juice

10 ml (2 t) orange juice

orange and lemon rind, cut into julienne strips

freshly chopped herbs

salt and freshly ground black pepper to taste

SALAD

500 g screw noodles

150 g courgettes, cut into pieces

150 g patty pans, cut into pieces

100 g carrots, sliced into julienne strips

100 g mangetout (snow peas)

150 g whole baby corn

200 g whole cherry tomatoes

olive oil

salt and freshly ground black pepper

Blend all the ingredients for the salad dressing in a screw-top jar, shake well and leave to stand for at least half an hour before using.

Cook the noodles in rapidly boiling salted water until tender, drain and rinse under cold running water.

Stir-fry all the vegetables in a little olive oil until glossy. Season to taste with salt and pepper. Place all the ingredients in a dish, moisten with the salad dressing and chill until needed.

Serves 6-8.

Moist chocolate cake

CAKE

250 ml (1 c) cocoa

250 ml (1 c) sour cream

3 extra-large eggs

430 ml (1¾ c) cake flour

5 ml (1 t) baking powder

2 ml (½ t) bicarbonate of soda

2 ml (½ t) salt

300 g soft butter

350 ml castor sugar

10 ml (2 t) vanilla essence

ICING

250 ml (1 c) fresh cream

500 g milk chocolate, broken into squares

Preheat the oven to 180 °C (350 °F). Grease a large 30-cm cake tin or two 20-cm cake tins with butter or margarine or spray with nonstick spray.

Mix the cocoa, sour cream and eggs until smooth. Sift together the cake flour, baking powder, bicarbonate of soda and salt. Beat the butter and castor sugar together until light and creamy. Add the dry ingredients and mix. Fold in the cocoa mixture and vanilla essence. Turn the batter into the prepared tin(s). Bake for about 40 minutes or until done and a skewer comes out clean when inserted in the centre of the cake. Turn out onto a wire rack to cool.

Slowly bring the cream to the boil, add the chocolate and stir until all the chocolate has melted and the mixture thickens. Cool slightly. If baking two cakes, sandwich the layers together with some of the icing and cover the cake with the remaining icing.

Makes 1 large cake.

Hetta van der Merwe of Paarl started hosting offal evenings to promote her catering business, but now people phone her regularly to find out when she will be holding another one. She was a city girl who ended up on a farm in the Karoo, says Hetta. Their farm was near the small village of Philipstown, where there were no restaurants. On Sundays, or during the hunting season, she frequently had to entertain twenty to thirty adult friends, and the same number of children, at a time. She knew nothing about cooking offal, so she had to learn fast. Here, in Paarl, she serves anything from curried and "vaal" offal to baked sheep's heads, as well as venison pie and farm-style vegetables. To add a Boland flavour, she cooks waterblommetjie bredie (stew) with a Malay lemon pudding for dessert. Starters include snoek pâté with brown bread, soup and skilpadjies. Boerekos with a twist, she calls it.

Brown bread with linseed

750 ml (3 c) whole-wheat flour
750 ml (3 c) cake flour
10 g (1 packet) instant yeast
250 ml (1 c) linseed
125 ml (½ c) rolled wheat
10 ml (2 t) salt
20 ml (4 t) sugar
1-1,5 litres (4-6 c) lukewarm water

Mix all the ingredients together, adding water a little at a time until the mixture resembles clotted cream. Divide the dough between three greased coffee tins – the 750 g size (fill them three quarters full) – and leave to rise for 1 hour in a warm place. Meanwhile, preheat the oven to 180 °C (350 °F).

Push the handle of a wooden spoon into the centre of the dough to knock it back slightly and place the tins in the oven. Bake for 1 hour and then for another 20-30 minutes at 150 °C (300 °F).

Cool the loaves in the tins for 10 minutes before turning out carefully on a tea towel. (Do not shake the tins as the loaves will crack.) Leave to cool before serving. Makes 3 small loaves.

Snoek pâté

5 ml (1 t) curry powder
1 medium onion, chopped
250 g (1 tub) creamed cottage cheese
about 500 g flaked smoked snoek
1 medium potato, peeled, cooked
  and mashed
salt and lemon pepper

Process all the ingredients in a food processor for 1-2 minutes until well blended. Season to taste and spoon into small dishes. Serve with brown bread.
Serves 6.

Brown bread with linseed and snoek pâté (in front)

Venison pie

a little oil

500 g lamb shanks or rib

2 kg venison with bone, preferably springbok

1 medium onion, studded with 10 whole
   cloves

10 ml (2 t) crushed garlic

800 ml hot water

250 ml (1 c) red wine or 125 ml (½ c) grape
   vinegar

15 ml (1 T) salt

5 ml (1 t) freshly ground black pepper

20 ml (4 t) Bisto powder (gravy thickener),
   mixed with 20 ml (4 t) water

1 roll frozen puff pastry, thawed

beaten egg yolk

Heat about 15 ml (1 T) oil in a heavy-based saucepan and lightly brown the lamb for 5-10 minutes. Remove from the saucepan, then lightly brown the venison. Remove from the saucepan and pour off the excess fat. Fry the onion and garlic until glossy. Return the meat to the saucepan and pour over the water and red wine. Cover and simmer slowly for 3 hours until the meat falls off the bone. Season with salt and pepper. Remove the bones and thicken the sauce with the Bisto paste. Spoon the meat into a large pie dish and cool.

Preheat the oven to 200 °C (400 °F). Roll out the pastry until slightly thinner and place over the meat. Pierce the pastry in a few places to allow the steam to escape. Brush with beaten egg yolk and decorate with designs cut out of the pastry.

Bake for about 20 minutes until golden brown and done. Serves 8-10.

"Vaal" offal

1 well-scrubbed offal
salt and freshly ground black pepper
30-45 ml (2-3 T) lemon juice
5 large potatoes, peeled and cubed

Rinse the offal well and cut the tripe into pieces. Place in a saucepan and season well with salt, black pepper and lemon juice. Add just enough water to cover. Cover the saucepan and simmer slowly for 4-6 hours. Add the potatoes an hour before the end of the cooking time and simmer until tender. Mash two of the potatoes in the gravy to thicken it.

Serves 6.

Curried offal

"vaal" offal (see recipe)
2-3 onions, sliced
1 clove garlic, crushed
25 ml (5 t) oil
about 45 ml (3 T) mild curry powder
pinch ground cumin (optional)
10 ml (2 t) turmeric
a generous pinch of dried mixed herbs
a dash of vinegar
15 ml (1 T) apricot jam

Prepare the "vaal" offal as described and simmer until just before the potatoes are added.

Fry the onions and garlic in the oil until tender and fragrant. Add the curry powder, ground cumin and turmeric and fry for 2 minutes. Add the herbs, vinegar and apricot jam and add to the offal along with the potatoes. Simmer until tender and flavoursome. Season with more salt and pepper if necessary.

Serve with rice, chutney and vegetables.

Serves 6.

Curried offal (left) and "vaal" offal (right front)

Lemon pudding

100 ml butter

125 ml (½ c) castor sugar

2 extra-large eggs, separated

250 ml (1 c) self-raising flour

pinch salt

grated rind and juice of
 1 large lemon

500 ml (2 c) milk

Preheat the oven to 180 °C (350 °F) and lightly grease a medium-sized oven dish with butter or margarine or spray with nonstick spray.

Beat the butter and sugar together until light and fluffy and add in the egg yolks one by one, beating well after each addition. Sift the flour and salt together and fold into the egg mixture, alternating with the lemon juice and rind and 250 ml (1 c) milk. Beat the egg whites until soft peaks form and fold in. Add the remaining milk, mix lightly and turn the batter into the greased dish. Bake for 30-40 minutes until just set and cool slightly.

Serve lukewarm with a thin custard.

Serves 6-8.

Laetitia Prinsloo, owner of The Institute of Culinary Arts, has a romantic streak; responsible, perhaps, for her choice of pink Christmas buffet for You. She believes food is an art form and a reflection of one's personality. She says we should stop imitating other countries and prepare what is appropriate to our hot climate. The quality of our fresh produce is every bit as good as that of anything found in France, she assures us. And, she feels, given the drive displayed by the country's youth, we can achieve anything. We should use what is available locally: the proteas and roses were obtained in the area; so were the berries, strawberries and fruit – perfect for a joyful Christmas, dressed in pink, with plenty of our own fruit and flavours.

CHRISTMAS BUFFET

Preferably the table should be prepared outdoors. Cover a wooden table with a long, white runner and arrange all the food, on large white platters and dishes, on it. This meal serves 10-12 people.

Iced strawberry soup

Refreshingly cool and creamy at the same time – an amazing soup!

250 g fresh strawberries
500 ml (2 c) rosé wine
250 ml (1 c) strawberry yoghurt
125 ml (½ c) cream
freshly ground black pepper
   and a pinch of sugar

Rinse and halve the strawberries. Marinate them in the wine overnight. Pour into a saucepan the next day and simmer for about 20 minutes until tender. Cool and chill. Purée the mixture, add the yoghurt and cream, and season to taste with black pepper and sugar.
   Serve cold with ice cubes.

Christmas duck with couscous and dried figs

STUFFING
375 ml (1½ c) couscous
1 large onion, chopped
3 cloves garlic, crushed
oil
250 g dried figs, sliced
10-15 ml (2-3 t) freshly chopped
   mixed herbs, e.g. thyme, sage
   and parsley
200 ml red wine
30 ml (2 T) balsamic vinegar
salt and freshly ground black
   pepper

1 duck, about 2 kg
salt and freshly ground black
   pepper
butter and oil for cooking

Preheat the oven to 180 °C (350 °F). Grease an oven pan well with butter or margarine or spray with nonstick spray.
   Prepare the couscous according to the instructions on the packet and set aside. Sauté the onion and garlic in a little oil until tender. Add the figs and herbs and sauté for another minute. Add the wine and vinegar and bring to the boil. Remove from the heat and stir in the couscous. Season to taste with salt and black pepper and leave to cool.
   Remove as much of the fat inside the duck cavity as possible. Season the cavity with salt and black pepper and stuff with the couscous mixture. Truss the duck and cover with a little butter and oil. Oven-roast for 1-2 hours, turning the bird every 20 minutes. Baste with the pan juices.
   Serve with green fig preserve grilled over the coals.

Fresh fruit in ginger syrup

GINGER SYRUP

500 g sugar

1 litre (4 c) water

1 lemon

1 orange

4-cm piece fresh ginger, skinned
   and grated

berry vinegar to taste

1 small watermelon

1 winter melon

1 sweetmelon (spanspek)

fresh mint leaves, chopped

Stir the sugar and water over low heat until the sugar has dissolved. Add the remaining ingredients for the syrup, except the vinegar, and boil rapidly until syrupy, about 1 hour.

Cool and remove the lemon and orange. Add berry .vinegar to taste.

Use a melon baller to scoop out balls from all the fruit (equal quantities of each). Place the fruit balls in the cooled syrup, add the mint leaves and mix. Chill for 1-2 hours before serving.

Serve with gammon in ginger ale.

Gammon in ginger ale

3-3,5 kg boned gammon

2-3 litres ginger ale

1 medium onion, sliced

a few bay leaves

6 black peppercorns

6 whole cloves

4-cm piece fresh ginger, skinned
   and chopped

GLAZE

whole cloves

75 ml (5 T) ginger preserve,
   finely chopped

20 ml (4 t) ginger syrup

Soak the gammon in cold water for 4-6 hours before cooking. Drain and place the gammon in a large saucepan. Add the ginger ale and remaining ingredients. Cover and bring to the boil. Reduce the heat. Calculate the cooking time, allowing 25 minutes per 500 g meat. Simmer slowly until done. Remove the gammon from the cooking liquid and cool. Remove the rind.

Preheat the oven to 180 °C (350 °F). Grease a large oven pan well with butter or margarine or use a nonstick spray.

Using a sharp knife, cut diamond shapes in the fatty layer of the meat. Insert a clove in the centre of each diamond. Place the meat in the oven pan. Mix the chopped ginger and ginger syrup and carefully spread a thick layer over the meat. Oven-roast for 40-45 minutes until the meat is lightly browned and glazed. Baste frequently with extra ginger syrup.

Serve hot or cold with fresh fruit in ginger syrup.

Chicken liver mould

100 ml white wine

100 ml port

50 ml brandy

50 ml chopped onion

3 cloves garlic, crushed

a few sprigs thyme

400 g chicken livers

5 extra-large eggs

400 g butter, melted

salt and freshly ground
   black pepper to taste

Preheat the oven to 150 °C (300 °F). Line an oblong, ovenproof ceramic dish or loaf tin, about 12 cm x 21 cm, with plastic wrap.

Bring the wine, port, brandy, onion, garlic and thyme to the boil. Simmer to reduce the liquid to about a third. Remove the thyme and cool slightly.

Rinse the livers under cold running water and remove all membranes. Purée in a food processor until smooth and add the eggs one at a time while the machine is running. Add the wine mixture and butter and blend well. Season generously with salt and black pepper. Press through a sieve and turn into the prepared dish. Cover with a lid or aluminium foil and place in an oven pan filled halfway with boiling water.

Bake for 20-30 minutes (depending on the thickness of the dish) until set but still soft. Leave the dish to cool in the oven pan and chill in the fridge overnight. Unmould onto a serving platter just before serving.

Smoked gammon in ginger ale with fresh fruit in ginger syrup

Stuffed strawberries

This is a winner.

125 g blueberries, fresh or frozen

60 g pecan nuts, coarsely chopped

100 ml port

1 cinnamon stick

brown sugar to taste

freshly ground black pepper

about 1 kg fresh strawberries, rinsed

Place the blueberries, pecan nuts, port, cinnamon stick and brown sugar in a saucepan and simmer over low heat for 10-15 minutes. Season with black pepper. Cool and chill in the fridge. Remove the cinnamon stick.

Hull the strawberries and carefully hollow them out with a small knife. Spoon a little of the stuffing into each strawberry. Serve cold.

Frozen fruit filled with fruity ice cream

Fill fresh fruit with ice cream and freeze to coat with a frosty layer.

FRUITY ICE CREAM

100 g sugar

100 ml water

3 egg yolks

300 ml cream

450 ml fruit purée

any fresh fruit in season

Dissolve the sugar in the water and boil until the syrup reaches the thread stage. Beat the egg yolks and slowly add the syrup while beating continuously. Continue beating until the mixture is light and fluffy and the dish feels cold. Fold in the cream and beat well. Finally add the fruit purée and turn the mixture into a freezer-proof container. Place in the freezer until the mixture starts freezing around the edges. Beat with a wire beater and freeze once more. Repeat the process 3-4 times. Line the surface of the ice cream with wax paper to prevent the formation of ice crystals and freeze until required.

Remove the tops and stems of the fruit and set aside. Hollow out the fruit and fill with the ice cream. Replace the cut-off tops to form a lid and freeze the fruit until hard. Arrange on a serving platter and serve.

Frozen fruit filled with fruity ice cream (left) and stuffed strawberries (right)

At Riverside, outside Simondium, fresh fruit is used to prepare unforgettable festive meals. Our hostess, Wilna Rabe, believes in honest food, served attractively. The alfresco meal she planned for us has the advantage that it can be served either hot or cold. If you prefer the meal hot, you can add rice or potatoes to the menu.

Grape jam

2 kg grapes, halved and seeds removed
250 ml (1 c) water
2 kg sugar (if using hanepoot grapes,
   use 750 g sugar for every 1 kg grapes)
30 ml (2 T) lemon juice

Boil the grapes in the water until just tender. Layer the grapes and sugar in a saucepan and leave overnight. Add the lemon juice (15 ml (1 T) for every 1 kg fruit) and proceed as described for the plum or nectarine jam (p. 121).
   Enough for about 3-4 honey jars.

A festive meal with fresh fruit curry salsa (behind left), p. 122, grilled chicken wings (front left), p. 123, plum and pear mustard (centre), p. 122, and leg of lamb (far right)

Plum or nectarine jam

For years Mienie Abrahams has been the mainstay in Riverside's kitchen. Thanks to her the shelves are always well stocked with a variety of jams. Use the orchard run – top-quality fruit that's discarded – to make jam. Enjoy it with fresh bread.

2 kg fruit such as plums or nectarines, stoned (retain the skins) and diced

500 ml (2 c) water

2 kg sugar

15 ml (1 T) lemon juice

1 piece crushed ginger

Boil the fruit and water until the fruit is just tender – the back of a match must easily pierce the skin of the fruit. Add the blanched pips to the mixture. Remove the saucepan from the heat and add the sugar. Stir well and leave until all the sugar has dissolved. Add the lemon juice and ginger, return the saucepan to the heat and boil slowly for about 45 minutes until the jam is ready. Scoop off the scum that forms on top of the mixture and stir occasionally. To test if the jam is ready, Wilna spoons a little of the jam on a saucer. If the jam feels like honey – it feels as if the spoon slides over the saucer – the jam is ready. Spoon the jam into clean, sterilised jars and store in a cool place.

Enough for about 3-4 honey jars.

Sparkling pear punch

50 ml sugar

100 ml lemon juice

6 firm pears, peeled and cored

500 ml (2 c) fruit juice mixture (peach, pear and plum juice)

1-2 bottles (750 ml each) dry white wine

1 bottle (750 ml) sparkling grape juice

Heat the sugar and lemon juice, stirring to dissolve the sugar before the mixture comes to the boil. Simmer until a syrup is formed.

Pour boiling water over the pears and leave for a short while. Drain and dice the pears. Pour the sugar syrup over the pears, add the fruit juice mixture and white wine and chill until needed. Add the sparkling grape juice just before serving.

Serve with ice and decorate with sprigs of fresh mint and lemon verbena, if preferred.

Serves 6.

Sparkling pear punch

Plum and pear mustard

The recipe for this mustard comes from Italy, says Wilna. Serve with duck, chicken, turkey and pasta.

6 plums, stoned and skinned

3 pears, cored and skinned

125 ml (½ c) grape vinegar (use white vinegar
  for yellow plums and red vinegar for red plums)

45 ml (3 T) fruit juice mixture (pear, grape
  and peach juice)

about 250 ml (1 c) sugar

3 whole cloves

5 ml (1 t) cardamom

2 ml (½ t) ground cinnamon

pinch salt

rind of ½ lemon

60 ml (4 T) Dijon mustard

Purée the fruit and place in a saucepan. Add the vinegar, fruit juice, sugar and all the seasonings, except the mustard. Heat slowly while stirring continuously until the sugar has dissolved. Simmer gently until the mixture is nice and thick and no longer watery. Add the mustard, discard the whole spices and purée once more in the food processor if you prefer a smooth mustard. Spoon into a clean jar.

Makes about 250 ml (1 c).

Fresh fruit curry salsa

Use a variety of fresh fruit – pears, plums, nectarines, and grapes. Plunge the fruit in cold water with a few vitamin C tablets to prevent discoloration. Alternatively, sprinkle the fruit with lemon juice. Serve the fruit curry with a roast leg of lamb, chicken or venison.

6 pieces preserved ginger

2 onions, finely chopped

60 ml (¼ c) butter

15 ml (1 T) curry powder

15 ml (1 T) cake flour

5 ml (1 t) coriander seeds

500 ml (2 c) chicken stock

10 ml (2 t) lemon juice

salt and freshly ground black pepper to taste

750 ml (3 c) desiccated coconut

1,25 litres (5 c) fresh fruit, stoned (retain skins)
  and cut into pieces

Plunge the pieces of ginger into boiling water to remove most of the syrup, drain and chop finely. Sauté the onions in butter until tender, add the curry, cake flour, coriander seeds and ginger and heat slowly for about 5 minutes while stirring continuously. Remove from the heat, slowly stir in the chicken stock, return the saucepan to the stove and bring to the boil.

Add the lemon juice and salt and pepper to taste. Simmer for about 30 minutes. Remove from the heat and stir in the coconut. Add the fruit and mix. Chill until needed.

Serves 6.

*Roast leg of lamb served with
fresh fruit curry salsa (back)*

Grilled chicken wings

Wilna's husband, Frikkie, likes to grill chicken wings over the coals. He snaps each wing at the joint and threads it onto a skewer. Pour your favourite marinade over the wings, sprinkle with a little peri-peri, add a sprig of fresh rosemary and leave for about 30 minutes. Grill high above the coals until brown and done. Serve hot or cold with the plum and pear mustard (see recipe on p. 122).

Grape cheesecake

Aunt Helene van der Westhuizen is indispensable at Riverside and often bakes this cheesecake for the guesthouse. It makes enough for 18 servings.

CRUST

⅔ of a 200-g packet disgestive biscuits, crushed

15-30 ml (1-2 T) margarine or butter, melted

FILLING

1 packet (80 g) lemon jelly

250 ml (1 c) boiling water

2 containers (250 g each) smooth cottage cheese

125 ml (½ c) castor sugar

juice of 2 lemons

250 ml (1 c) cream

TOPPING

red grapes, halved

3 ml (generous ½ t) gelatine

125 ml (½ c) red grape juice

Mix the crushed biscuits and melted margarine or butter and press into the base of a 23-cm loose-bottomed cake tin.

Dissolve the lemon jelly in the boiling water and cool, but do not allow to set.

Beat the cottage cheese, sugar and lemon juice until well blended. Add the cream and beat well. Slowly add the jelly while beating continuously. Pour the mixture into the prepared crust and chill until set.

Arrange the grapes on top of the filling. Dissolve the gelatine in a little grape juice. Heat until just melted, mix with the remaining grape juice and pour over. Chill until set.

Makes a large cake.

Valley of
abundance

Surrounded by azure mountains and boasting fynbos in the veld, vast vineyards and orchards as far as the eye can see, the beauty of the Breede River valley refreshes the soul and gratifies the eye. Masses of yellow cannas and bougainvillea line the roads to the wine estates, gardens are covered with roses and jacarandas shade the streets.

The Breede River is the lifeblood of the valley; farms extend along its banks and the fertile soil is planted mostly with grapes that produce quality wines.

Among the unspoilt mountains with their fynbos and imposing rock formations, where klipspringers, porcupines and even leopards still roam freely, it's the game tracks on the path, the fragrance of the veld and the fresh breeze caressing your skin that bring peace to mind and soul. But, above all, it's the warm friendliness of the valley's inhabitants that sticks in your memory, their good-natured hospitality that makes you feel at home.

Robertson is known as a town for all seasons; it has many attractions, not the least of which are its temperate climate, good wines, abundant fruit, thoroughbred horses and clean air.

It was this attractive, tree-filled town full of friendly people, that made them decide to retire here, says Joan van den Heever, who lives in Van Riebeeck Street. When they moved here, their pace of living slowed down; they had more time to think about the really important things in life, time simply to stand and look at the flowers, and time to listen to the townspeople who love to chat and have a gift for turning something insignificant into an entertaining story.

Around Robertson the farms – most of them inherited and in the family for generations – stretch across hills to the foothills of the Langeberg and Sonderend Mountains. This is mainly wine country, but there are also numerous orchards of deciduous fruit destined for local and overseas markets. In spring the fragrance of blossoms is in the air, and in summer the branches bend under the weight of sun-ripened fruit.

Most of the present farmers belong to a younger generation. They continue the wine-making tradition with pride, while their wives prepare dishes to complement the wines and serve them elegantly and with style.

In the Stettyns Mountains, outside Worcester, we learnt anew to appreciate the wonders of nature: unspoilt mountains and deep ravines, sandstone formations covered with ancient lichens and, in the veld, ericas, proteas, kalkoentjies, blue sage and dassiekruid. We picnicked on the highest peaks and looked out over the dam and scrub veld.

Today, in the Breede River valley, you can visit tasting venues and cafés, guest farms and mountain resorts, and even take a trip on a river boat; you can sample food and wine and at the same time enjoy the scenic beauty around you.

Joan van den Heever says she's learnt a great deal since settling in Robertson. There's an abundance of fresh fruit and vegetables in the valley, and nothing is ever wasted. While the fruit is available provision must be made for later, so everyone preserves it in some form or other – from citron preserve to lemon and granadilla syrup. Recently, she dried some peaches on a corrugated iron roof.

Tuna mould

Served with fresh whole-wheat bread, this tuna mould makes a wonderful light lunch, says Joan. Make it a day in advance for best results.

1 packet (about 18 ml) gelatine

15 ml (1 T) cold water

100 ml boiling water

2 tins (170 g each) tuna, drained

1 large onion, finely chopped

200 ml mayonnaise

100 ml tomato sauce

180 ml (¾ c) plain yoghurt

10 ml (2 t) sugar (optional)

salt and freshly ground black pepper to taste

Line a small loaf tin with plastic wrap. Soak the gelatine in the cold water until spongy. Add the boiling water, stirring until the gelatine has dissolved. Flake the tuna until fine and mix with the rest of the ingredients. Season to taste with salt and pepper. Add the gelatine and turn the mixture into the prepared loaf tin. Chill until set.

Serve with whole-wheat bread and slices of lemon. Serves 4-6.

Lemon syrup

12 lemons
2,5 kg sugar
1 packet (15 g) tartaric acid
1 packet (15 g) Epsom salts
1 packet (15 g) cream of tartar
1,5 litres (6 c) boiling water

Wash the lemons and grate the rind carefully. Squeeze out the juice and add to the rind. Add the rest of the ingredients. Stir until the sugar has dissolved and leave overnight. The next day, strain the syrup through a muslin cloth or fine sieve (using a muslin cloth results in a clearer syrup) and pour into clean bottles.

Serve mixed with ice-cold water or soda water.

Makes about 2 litres (8 c) of syrup.

Granadilla syrup

7 x 250 ml (7 c) sugar
1,5 litres (6 c) water
500 ml (2 c) granadilla pulp
1 packet (15 g) tartaric acid
1 packet (15 g) Epsom salts

Dissolve the sugar in the water and add the granadilla pulp. Boil the mixture for 5 minutes. Remove from the heat and strain through a sieve, stirring the pulp with a wooden spoon to separate the flesh from the pips and to remove all the juice. Return a few pips to the syrup, add the tartaric acid and Epsom salts and bring to the boil once more, stirring well to dissolve the last two ingredients. Rinse a few bottles well with boiling water and pour the hot syrup into the bottles. Seal.

Serve with ice-cold water or soda water. (This syrup will last for at least a year.)

Makes about 2 litres (8 c) syrup.

Cape fruit tart

Brenda Baumgarten, who also lives in Van Riebeeck Street, has always loved cooking. She previously did product development for a company, a position made possible by her domestic science background. This tart, with its combination of fresh and tinned fruit, is her personal favourite. Her mother-in-law, Bettie, gave her the recipe and Brenda's been making it for years.

PASTRY

375 g (2⅔ c) cake flour

15 ml (1 T) baking powder

250 g sugar

375 g cold butter

FILLING

4 bananas, sliced

1 tin (740 g) pie apples

½ pineapple, peeled and thinly sliced

1 tin (410 g) peach halves

80 ml (⅓ c) chopped pecan nuts

60 ml (¼ c) fruitcake mix

juice of ½ lemon

cinnamon, nutmeg and sugar to taste

Preheat the oven to 200 °C (400 °F).

Sift the cake flour and baking powder together and add the sugar. Grate the butter and, using your fingertips, rub it into the dry ingredients until well mixed. Press two-thirds of the pastry into the base and along the sides of a large pie dish and chill the rest of the pastry.

To make the filling, divide each ingredient in half and arrange alternating layers of bananas, pie apples, pineapple and peach halves in the dish. Sprinkle with the nuts and fruitcake mix. Sprinkle the lemon juice on top and flavour judiciously with cinnamon, nutmeg and sugar. Repeat the layers and grate the rest of the pastry on top. Bake for about an hour, or until the pie crust is done and golden brown. Serve hot or cold with whipped cream if desired.

Makes 1 large tart.

Suurtjies

During our visit to Robertson Joan van den Heever also let us sample suurtjies, Robertson's own delicacy made with early apricots. They have a wonderful sweet-and-sour almond flavour and can be served on their own or enjoyed with ice cream.

4 kg firm apricots
2,5 kg sugar
500 ml (2 c) white vinegar

Wash the apricots well. Using a small fork, prick holes all over the fruit. Soak the apricots in salted water. Drain well and allow to dry. Place the apricots in a plastic bowl and cover with the sugar. Add the vinegar and cover the bowl with plastic wrap. Allow the apricots to stand overnight.

Drain the fruit the next day, reserving the sugar and vinegar syrup that has formed overnight. Pour the syrup into a stainless-steel saucepan and bring to the boil. Pour this hot syrup over the apricots and cover with a plate, ensuring the apricots are completely immersed in the syrup. Leave overnight once more. Repeat this process five times. The syrup may turn dark towards the end of the process, but this is normal. On the sixth day, bring the syrup to the boil once more and add the fruit. Simmer for a while if softer fruit is preferred. Transfer the fruit to sterilised glass jars, add the syrup and seal immediately. Turn the jars upside down and store in a cool place for three months. Allow to mature and for the sweet-and-sour almond flavour to develop.

Makes 4 kg suurtjies.

Decadent cheesecake

The blackboard in front of De(café)nated in Church Street invites you for cappuccino and cake, and here you will find the most delectable cheesecake. Lihan Odendal, originally from Robertson, made his home in Cape Town for a while before returning to open his coffee shop in his home town. The light and dark layers of this cheesecake not only look fabulous, but the chocolate layer also gives it a heavenly taste. The cake contains no eggs.

CRUST
125 g butter or margarine
2 packets (200 g each)
  Tennis biscuits, crushed

FILLING
3 containers (250 g each)
  smooth cottage cheese
2 tins (397 g each)
  condensed milk
125 ml (½ c) lemon juice
250 ml (1 c) sugar
10 ml (2 t) custard powder
250 ml (1 c) cream, chilled
  and stiffly whipped
90 ml (6 T) cocoa

Preheat the oven to 180 °C (350 °F). Grease a 23-cm loose-bottomed or springform cake tin with butter or margarine or spray with nonstick spray.

To make the crust, melt the butter and stir in the crumbs. Press the mixture onto the base and sides of the prepared tin and chill until needed.

To make the filling, mix all the ingredients together, except the cream and cocoa. Fold in the cream and pour half the mixture into the crust. Sift the cocoa into the rest of the cottage cheese mixture and carefully pour on top. Bake for 30 minutes until pale brown around the edges. Remove from the oven and allow to cool. Chill until set. Place on a serving platter and remove the springform rim carefully.

Makes a large cheesecake.

Decadent cheesecake

Spinach tramezzini

Café Rosa's plants and trees create a green oasis next to the station at the entrance to Robertson. The stationmaster's former house is now Willie and Hilda le Roux's nursery, and also their home. Their children, Liandri and Deon, run a coffee shop among the plants, where guests can relax under umbrellas in the garden. Their tramezzinis and salads, in particular, are very popular.

2 rashers cooked bacon, shredded

2-3 spinach leaves, shredded and
   sautéed in olive oil with garlic

1 round feta cheese, crumbled

a few slices mozzarella cheese

1 focaccia, halved

4 slices tomato

Mix the bacon, spinach and feta cheese and set aside. Arrange the mozzarella cheese on the bottom half of the focaccia. Top with the tomato slices and stack the spinach mixture on top. Cover with the top half of the focaccia and grill under the oven grill or in a toasted-sandwich maker until the bread is lightly browned and the cheese has just melted.

Makes 1 tramezzini.

A visit to Philip and Almien du Toit at their farm Wederom lasts well into the night. We heard all about the family names and nicknames – to make it easier to distinguish between the namesakes – and, at the same time, were told entertaining stories about past feuds over spring water. Almien has a lovely garden, and one is inclined to believe her when she says that fairies live in it. Hanepoot Huisie is quite near the homestead. Previously a shop where people bought their newspapers and petrol, it now serves as a resting place for weary guests. Almien's breakfast trays feature treats such as muesli and yoghurt; sliced ham and achar; home-made breads; and broccoli muffins with jams and cheese.

Broccoli muffins

Almien was given this recipe by Mimmie du Toit of La Maison, a cousin of hers who's married to one of Philip's cousins.

375 ml (1½ c) cooked broccoli,
   finely chopped

250 ml (1 c) chopped ham

125 ml (½ c) grated Cheddar cheese

1 onion, finely chopped

6 extra-large eggs

125 ml (½ c) oil

300 ml cake flour

12,5 ml (2½ t) baking powder

5 ml (1 t) dried origanum

5 ml (1 t) dried parsley

1 ml (¼ t) dried thyme

1 ml (¼ t) garlic salt

Preheat the oven to 200 °C (400 °F). Grease the hollows of a muffin pan well with butter or margarine or spray with nonstick spray.

Mix the broccoli, ham, cheese and onion. Beat the eggs until foaming and add the oil. Sift the dry ingredients together, add to the egg mixture along with the broccoli mixture and mix. Fill the hollows of the muffin pan with the mixture and bake for about 25-30 minutes or until done and a skewer comes out clean when inserted into the centre of the muffin. Remove the muffins from the pan, allow to cool slightly and serve lukewarm with cheese.

Makes 8 medium muffins.

Tapioca pudding

On the Zeeman family farm Aunt Mimmie Zeeman's favourite dishes are still prepared for family get-togethers. She lived on Goudmyn for 36 years and raised eight children. Her legendary recipes for hanepoot grape pie, and bread and tapioca puddings are passed on from one generation to the next, says Ina Zeeman, who now lives on Goudmyn.

250 ml (1 c) tapioca
1,5 litres (6 c) milk
1 ml (¼ t) salt
2 large pieces stick
  cinnamon
310 ml (1¼ c) sugar
3-4 large eggs (250 g)
a little butter

Soak the tapioca in 1 litre milk overnight. The next morning, add the salt and cinnamon and cook slowly over very low heat until the tapioca is soft and translucent (a double boiler is ideal for this, but the tapioca can also be cooked in the microwave oven). Add some of the remaining milk if necessary. Stir the mixture occasionally while cooking. Remove from the heat when cooked, stir in the rest of the milk and the sugar, stirring until the sugar has dissolved. Allow to cool until lukewarm. Beat the eggs and stir into the tapioca mixture. Pour into a greased ovenproof dish, dot with butter if preferred and bake for about 1 hour or until set in an oven preheated to 180 °C (350 °F). Serve hot or lukewarm.
    Serves 6.

Fraai Uitzicht is situated on the slopes of the Langeberg, overlooking the beautiful Klaas Voogds valley, near Robertson. This historic wine farm dates back to 1798. Mario Motti and Axel Spanholtz renovated the old homestead and turned it into a guest farm, with four guest cottages and its own restaurant. They serve their own wine with the superb dishes Mario prepares. The herbs, vegetables and salad greens all come fresh from their vegetable garden. The menu is varied and has an interesting international flavour.

Oven-roasted vegetables

about 250 ml (1 c) coarsely cut
  vegetables, e.g. carrots, potatoes,
  sweet potatoes and turnips
olive oil
salt
freshly ground black pepper
balsamic vinegar

Preheat the oven to 200 °C (400 °F). Sprinkle the vegetables with olive oil and season with salt. Oven-roast for about an hour until cooked and tender. Season with freshly ground black pepper and sprinkle generously with balsamic vinegar.
    Serve with the stuffed pork fillet (p. 135).

Stuffed pork fillet with roasted vegetables

RED WINE SAUCE

400 ml red wine

1 onion, chopped

2 sprigs fresh rosemary

20 ml (4 t) cornflour

125 ml (½ c) pear and apple juice

50 g (½ packet) hazelnuts, toasted
   and finely chopped

sugar, salt and pepper to taste

15 ml (1 T) plain yoghurt

about 600 g pork fillet

salt and freshly ground black pepper

olive oil for frying

STUFFING

1 onion, finely chopped

1 clove garlic, crushed

10 ml (2 t) butter

about 150 g rocket or baby spinach, shredded

Pour the wine into a saucepan, add the onion and rosemary and boil rapidly until reduced by half. Strain through a sieve. Mix the cornflour with the fruit juice and stir into the red wine sauce. Bring to the boil while stirring continuously. Stir in the hazelnuts and season with sugar, salt and pepper to taste. Remove from the heat and stir in the yoghurt. Keep warm.

Halve the fillet, but don't cut all the way through. Open it up, flattening it. Season with salt and pepper.

Sauté the onion and garlic in the butter until fragrant, add the rocket or spinach and heat until tender. Season with salt and pepper to taste. Spoon the mixture onto the fillet, close it again and secure with string or cocktail sticks. Heat a little olive oil in a frying pan and fry the fillet until brown all over, about 10 minutes a side. Cover and keep warm at 80 °C (180 °F) for up to an hour before serving.

To serve: Drizzle a little of the red wine sauce around the edge of the plate. Spoon the vegetables in the centre and surround with a few slices of fillet. Serve with green fig preserve.

Serves about 4.

Brothers Fred and Manie Viljoen of Viljoensdrift decided, after nearly thirty years, to reopen and renovate the old wine cellar and start making wine again. Fred, who has no formal training in wine-making, started experimenting in glass jars in his wife, Lindi's, kitchen. After numerous attempts he was satisfied, and some of their young wines have since won gold at the SA Young Wine Show.

The modern, yellow-painted tasting venue, with its blue cellar doors and enormous wooden deck, stands on the banks of the Breede River. The river boat, named Uncle Ben *after their father, is moored at the riverbank, ready to take guests out on the river.*

Lindi's food has a refreshing, modern touch. She likes to arrange cheeses, interesting salads and pâtés attractively on large platters. On the boat is a long table packed with food and, as the boat glides slowly along the river, you can look out for the rare clawless otter, see a river fish jump out of the water and feast your eyes on the beautiful birds and flowers of the Breede River valley.

Brie and green fig preserve surprise

Green fig preserve and Brie are a sublime combination, and this treat goes down well when tasting wine, says Lindi.

125 g Brie cheese

125 g cream cheese

5-6 preserved green figs, coarsely chopped

60 ml (¼ c) toasted almond flakes

Halve the Brie horizontally into two rounds. Mix the cream cheese with the green figs and almond flakes, and spread a little of the mixture on the bottom cheese layer. Place the remaining round of cheese on top and spread with the rest of the cream cheese mixture. Finish with extra toasted almond flakes.

Serves 6.

Stuffed pork fillet with roasted vegatables

Cheese truffles

150 g soft butter

250 g cream cheese

2-3 packets savoury biscuits
   (e.g. Tuc), coarsely crushed

50 g cashew nuts or walnuts, chopped

6 black olives, stoned and coarsely
   chopped

6 sun-dried tomatoes in oil, drained
   and coarsely chopped

toasted sesame seeds, poppy seeds
   and chopped parsley for rolling

Ensure the butter and cream cheese are equally soft. Combine the two, mixing well. Fold the biscuits, nuts, olives and sun-dried tomatoes into the mixture. Spoon the mixture into a flat dish and chill until firm. Cut into squares and roll each square into a ball. Roll the balls in the sesame seeds, poppy seeds or chopped parsley. Chill until firm and serve with a selection of other cheeses and Melba toast if preferred.

Makes about 30 truffles.

Marinated calamari, trout and anchovy salad

500 g frozen calamari rings

1 bottle French salad dressing

selection of fresh salad leaves

18 slices smoked trout or salmon

50 g capers

1 tin (50 g) rolled anchovy fillets

a few black olives

freshly ground black pepper

olive oil

fresh Parmesan cheese, grated
   or thinly sliced

Rinse the calamari and drain. Place in a dish and blanch in boiling water. Leave for about 1-2 minutes. Rinse under cold water, place in a clean jar and moisten with the salad dressing. Marinate overnight.

Arrange the salad leaves on a salad platter and arrange the trout and calamari on top. Add the capers, anchovy fillets and olives. Season with freshly ground black pepper and drizzle with olive oil. Finish with grated or sliced Parmesan cheese.

Makes a large salad.

Strawberry, bacon and spinach salad

a few young spinach leaves, well rinsed,
  stems removed, shredded

500 g strawberries, cut into pieces

125 g bacon, chopped

olive oil

60 ml (¼ c) balsamic vinegar

croutons

blue cheese, crumbled

Arrange the spinach leaves on a salad platter and arrange the strawberries on top. Fry the bacon in a little olive oil until crisp and scatter over the salad, adding the pan fat. Add the balsamic vinegar to the hot pan and return to the heat, loosening the coagulated cooking juices. Pour the hot vinegar over the salad and top with croutons and crumbled blue cheese.

Serves 4-6.

Smoked mackerel terrine

150 ml milk

1 small onion, cut into chunks

1 bay leaf

6 peppercorns

15 ml (1 T) butter

25 ml (5 t) cake flour

15 ml (1 T) gelatine

45 ml (3 T) cold water

45 ml (3 T) mayonnaise

150 ml cream cheese

2 hard-boiled eggs, coarsely
  chopped

225 g smoked mackerel, flaked

salt and freshly ground black pepper

juice and grated rind of ½ lemon

Line a small loaf tin with plastic wrap.

Heat the milk along with the onion, bay leaf and peppercorns. Set aside to steep. Melt the butter and stir in the flour. Strain the milk and stir into the flour mixture. Heat, stirring continuously, until the white sauce comes to the boil and thickens. Set aside to cool. Meanwhile, sprinkle the gelatine over the cold water and leave until it becomes spongy. Heat in the microwave oven or over boiling water until melted.

Add the mayonnaise and cream cheese to the cooled white sauce and mix. Add the eggs and mackerel. Season to taste with salt and pepper, lemon juice and rind. Add the melted gelatine and mix. Turn the mixture into the prepared loaf tin and chill overnight. Turn out onto a serving platter, remove the plastic wrap and garnish with watercress just before serving.

Makes 1 medium terrine.

Marinated sweet peppers

3 red sweet peppers, seeded and quartered

3 yellow sweet peppers, seeded and quartered

3 green sweet peppers, seeded and quartered

olive oil for brushing

60 ml (¼ c) olive oil

5 cloves garlic, crushed

30 ml (2 T) freshly squeezed lemon juice

30 ml (2 T) freshly chopped origanum, parsley
  or basil

salt and freshly ground black pepper to taste

8 anchovy fillets (optional)

a few peppadews (optional)

Preheat the oven grill. Place the sweet peppers on a baking sheet, skin side facing up, and brush with olive oil. Grill until the skins begin to blister and turn black. Place the sweet peppers in a plastic bag and close. Cool slightly in the bag, then remove the skins. Place the sweet peppers in a serving dish. Mix the olive oil with the garlic, lemon juice and herbs and season well with salt and black pepper. Pour over the sweet peppers and mix. Top with anchovy fillets and peppadews if preferred.

Serves 20 people as part of a buffet.

Onion straws

500 ml (2 c) cake flour
100 ml white onion soup powder
500 ml (2 c) grated Cheddar cheese
250 g butter, melted and cooled

Preheat the oven to 200 °C (400 °F).

Mix all the ingredients to form a dough and roll out until about 5 mm thick. Cut into long strips. Place on a greased baking sheet and bake for about 10-12 minutes until a pale straw colour.

Makes about 40 long, thin straws.

Port and chicken liver pâté

Lindi served this pâté in a pretty painted ceramic vase surrounded by spring onion sprigs.

100 g butter
500 g chicken livers, chopped
1 medium onion, chopped
2 cloves garlic, crushed
60 ml (¼ c) port
60 ml (¼ c) cream
15 ml (1 T) chopped chives
60 ml (¼ c) green peppercorns in
    brine, drained

Heat the butter in a large heavy-based saucepan. Add the chicken livers, onion and garlic and stir-fry over medium heat until the chicken livers are done but still slightly pink inside. Add the port, bring to the boil and simmer slowly for 5 minutes. Remove from the heat and cool slightly.

Place in a food processor and process until smooth, using the pulse action. Add the cream and process until everything has been mixed in. Spoon into a mixing bowl and add the chives and green peppercorns. Spoon into small ramekins and chill overnight.

Serve with parsley toast.

Makes about 500 g.

Onion straws with parsley toast (below left), port and chicken liver pâté (below right) and marinated biltong with fennel dip (far right)

Marinated biltong with fennel dip

FRENCH SALAD DRESSING

60 ml (¼ c) wine vinegar

125 ml (½ c) olive or salad oil

10 ml (2 t) salt

freshly ground black pepper to taste

60 ml (¼ c) chopped parsley

80 ml (⅓ c) chopped spring onion

500 g biltong, thinly sliced

FENNEL DIP

150 ml mayonnaise

150 ml sour cream

5 ml (1 t) chopped fresh fennel

1 small onion, very finely chopped

15 ml (1 T) chopped parsley

15 ml (1 T) lemon juice

1 ml (¼ t) mustard powder

salt and freshly ground black pepper
   to taste

Mix all the ingredients for the French salad dressing and pour over the biltong slices. Marinate for 4-6 hours. Drain and transfer the biltong to a small dish. Mix all the ingredients for the dip and serve with the marinated biltong.

Grilled sirloin in blue-cheese marinade

Besides producing award-winning wines, the Robertson Valley is also famous for its stud farms and thoroughbred horses. The stud farm Saratoga belongs to the Doms brothers, Henry and Fred. Henry's wife, Di, loves entertaining and also does catering. She was inspired by cookery courses she did with food expert Ina Paarman. This recipe for sirloin in blue-cheese marinade comes from her Ina Paarman collection. She specially prepared it for us in a Weber braai.

1 kg whole sirloin

5 ml (1 t) salt and pepper mixture

SAUCE

5 ml (1 t) beef stock powder

125 ml (½ c) blue-cheese salad dressing

30 ml (2 T) crumbled blue cheese

15 ml (1 T) espresso coffee granules

30 ml (2 T) boiling water

30 ml (2 T) whisky

Rub the sirloin well with the salt and pepper.

Mix the stock powder with the salad dressing and crumbled blue cheese. Dissolve the coffee granules in the boiling water and add to the sauce along with the whisky. Pour over the meat and marinate for at least 3-4 hours at room temperature.

Cook the meat in a Weber or gas braai. Grill the meat slowly over medium to hot coals until medium-done and still pink inside – about 40 minutes. Turn the meat frequently, basting with the marinade. Keep the lid on while cooking. Leave the sirloin to rest for 10 minutes before carving. Bring the rest of the marinade to the boil and serve with the meat together with a fresh green salad.

Serves 6.

From the highway you can see the road zigzagging high along the crest of the mountain. This is the 4x4 road of the new mountain resort, Klipbokkop, started by Gerhard and Elmarie Groenewald in the Stettyns Mountains on the far side of Worcester. During our visit, shortly after the opening in the winter of 2000, we went up the mountain in Land Cruisers – negotiating steep slopes and driving along hair-raising precipices, past Piet se Gat, through Grootkloof and Brandkloof to the Troonkamer, a name Elmarie gave this beautiful spot with its imposing rock formations and incredible views of the scrub veld, the plains and the Kwaggaskloof Dam, where we stopped for a picnic. Gerhard and Elmarie are nature lovers, and want to share their great love of the veld and for nature with others. Klipbokkop is not meant for 4x4 drivers only, but nature lovers who yearn for a little peace and quiet can also relax here.

We were treated to waterblommetjie bredie (stew) and quails straight from the Breede River valley, and Elmarie showed us how to make the most delectable pudding in a jiffy with a bottle of Amarula liqueur, fresh fruit and a cast-iron pan.

Vegetable loaf

Visitors can't get enough of this vegetable loaf served with a cheese pâté made with Bacon Kips.

250 ml (1 c) finely chopped onion
60 ml (¼ c) butter
625 ml (2½ c) self-raising flour
5 ml (1 t) salt
5 ml (1 t) dried mixed herbs
15 ml (1 T) freshly chopped parsley
625 ml (2½ c) scraped, coarsely grated
    carrots and courgettes
250 ml (1 c) grated Cheddar cheese
200 ml coarsely chopped pecan nuts
3 extra-large eggs
60 ml (¼ c) plain yoghurt or buttermilk

Preheat the oven to 180 °C (350 °F). Grease a medium-sized loaf tin with butter or margarine or spray with nonstick spray.

Sauté the onion in the butter until tender. Sift the self-raising flour and salt together. Add the herbs. Mix the onion, parsley, carrot-and-courgette mixture, cheese and nuts. Beat the eggs and yoghurt together. Sprinkle the flour mixture over the vegetable mixture, add the egg mixture and mix to bind all the ingredients, taking care not to overmix. Turn the mixture into the prepared loaf tin and bake for about 40 minutes, or until a skewer comes out clean when inserted into the centre of the loaf.

Serve with cheese pâté.
Makes 1 loaf.

Cheese pâté

1 container (250 g) smooth cottage
    cheese
30 ml (2 T) sandwich spread
15 ml (1 T) chutney
15 ml (1 T) mayonnaise
1 packet Bacon Kips biscuits
    (chive flavour), crushed

Mix the cottage cheese, sandwich spread, chutney and mayonnaise together. Add the crushed biscuits and mix. Chill until needed and serve with the vegetable loaf.
    Makes 250 ml (1 c) cheese pâté.

Cheese pâté

Klipbokkop's braaied snoek

Their guests are usually starving after a day in the mountains. Gerhard braais snoek over the coals, which they then serve with pot bread and grape jam.

1 fresh snoek, butterflied
salt
juice of 3 large lemons
250 g butter
freshly ground black pepper

Wash the snoek and leave it to dry in a windy area. Salt to taste. Heat the rest of the ingredients until the butter has melted. Place the snoek in a hinged grid fairly high above medium-hot coals, skin side facing down. After a short while, turn the snoek just to dry it. Then turn frequently, basting well with the lemon-butter mixture. Braai for 20 minutes at the most, depending on the thickness of the snoek. Cut into fillets and serve with pot bread and grape jam.
Serves 6-8.

Waterblommetjie bredie

In the Breede River Valley the farm dams are covered with waterblommetjies.

2,5 kg fresh waterblommetjies, thoroughly washed
   and stems removed if necessary
salted water
1-1,5 kg stewing mutton, such as neck or rib,
   cut into pieces
salt and freshly ground black pepper
2 medium onions, sliced
250 ml (1 c) water
12 baby potatoes
1 large cooking apple, cut into pieces
250 ml (1 c) white wine

Soak the waterblommetjies in salted water for a few hours. Drain, rinse and bring to a rapid boil in fresh water. Drain.

Season the meat with salt and pepper and brown in a heated black cast-iron pot or heavy-based saucepan. Add the onions and stir-fry until glossy. Add the water, cover and simmer slowly until partially cooked. Add the potatoes, waterblommetjies and apple, pour over the wine and simmer until the potatoes and waterblommetjies are cooked and tender. Season with salt and pepper. Do not stir too frequently as the waterblommetjies will become mushy. Serve with samp.

Serves 6.

Stuffed quails

At the Toontjies River quail farm they serve these birds in all kinds of interesting ways. For this dish, the quails are partially boned and stuffed. If you don't have a Weber, the quails can be covered with a large heat-resistant lid and cooked over medium-hot coals.

6 quails
salt and pepper
olive oil

STUFFING
125 ml (½ c) grated mozzarella cheese
125 ml (½ c) crumbled feta cheese
250 ml (1 c) steamed spinach, finely chopped
60 ml (¼ c) finely chopped almonds

Loosen the skin over the breastbone. Mix the ingredients for the stuffing and season with salt and pepper. Stuff the filling between the skin and the breastbone, taking care not to break the skin. Secure with a cocktail stick and season quails with salt and pepper.

Place the birds in a Weber, cover and braai over medium-hot coals for about 10 minutes. Turn, brush with olive oil and braai for another 15 minutes or until the quails are tender and nicely browned. Do not overcook.

Serves 4-6.

Caramelised fruit with Amarula liqueur

This dessert was concocted in a few minutes, using whatever ingredients were available in the kitchen at Klipbokkop.

125 ml (½ c) butter
125 ml (½ c) brown sugar
1 packet (200 g) marshmallows
250 ml (1 c) Amarula liqueur
50 ml orange and lemon juice
a few strawberries, halved
4 bananas, roughly sliced
3 oranges, cut into segments
rind of 2 lemons, cut into long, thin strips

Melt the butter and sugar over medium heat until caramelised. Stir occasionally. Add the marshmallows and heat, stirring continuously, until melted. Stir in the liqueur and juice and bring to the boil. Add the fruit and lemon rind and heat until warm. Do not allow the fruit to become soft. Serve hot with ice cream.

Serves 6.

Waterblommetjie bredie

Lunch break

From Cape Town, the N2 takes you across Sir Lowry's Pass to the South Coast, to pristine beaches and the warm blue waters of the Indian Ocean – desirable destinations for many a traveller. Fortunately, these days people are more inclined to stop along the way; to appreciate the beauty of the scenery and enjoy the delicacies each area has to offer. Many cars can be seen at farm stalls and roadside restaurants; these places are popular stops for travellers, but even city dwellers who want to get away from the hustle and bustle of urban life come here for breakfast or a home-cooked meal, then return to the city bearing delicious home-made delicacies.

When you reach the plateau on top of the Hottentots Holland Mountains you are among the apple orchards of the Cape. Elgin and Grabouw are well-known apple-farming centres and this fruit for the gods is plentiful at farm stalls. Emulating Europe with its numerous roadside restaurants, a coffee shop was combined with a farm stall, and the Orchard coffee shop, just outside Elgin, was born. When we visited it in 1997 we couldn't get enough of the mouthwatering open sandwiches, but it was their bewildering selection of cakes, tartlets and other baked treats that kept us at the counter, trying to make up our minds about what to have with our tea.

The road meanders on through the Overberg, across hills and valleys, flanked on either side by crops and peacefully grazing sheep. At the foot of the Langeberg is the town of Swellendam, with its rich heritage, that once again entices you to break your journey.

The Drostdy Museum, probably the oldest landmark in Swellendam, is situated on the outskirts of the town not far from the highway. The Zanddrift restaurant across the street also forms part of the museum complex. In this old farmhouse, dating back to 1795, the most delectable "mama's food" is prepared daily. Don't expect typically South African dishes, just mouthwatering food, lovingly prepared, in true Italian tradition.

In 1998 we went there for a day. There is no menu and the food is not served on individual plates. Each table gets its own platter of food and the guests help themselves. Local produce is used extensively: Swellendam's renowned youngberries go into the sauce for the cheesecake, and the stone-milled flour from the museum is used for baking scones. From the restaurant's garden come vegetables and herbs, and the veld provides wild mushrooms for the pot.

At Zanddrift Restaurant, next to the Drostdy Museum in Swellendam, Edwina Koehler provides home-cooked meals every day. She likes to chat to her guests first, to find out their food preferences – for the French she cooks to suit their taste, and the Italians are served food they prefer. She knows the British are quite undemanding and that she should never serve lamb to Americans. But she also serves South African dishes such as tomato bredie (stew), bean soup and cabbage friccadels.

First thing every morning, she goes shopping and then decides what to cook. Everything is freshly prepared each day, and she does all the cooking herself at the old hearth in the kitchen.

Meat salad

The salad forms part of the breakfast platter and is served with an omelette and a selection of cold meats.

220 g ham (or a variety or cold meats), diced

1 small onion, chopped

5 gherkins, chopped

160 ml (⅔ c) mayonnaise

10 ml (2 t) mustard powder

20 ml (4 t) chopped fresh parsley

salt and pepper

Mix the meat, onion and gherkins. Season the mayonnaise with the mustard and parsley, season to taste with salt and pepper and lightly mix with the meat. Serve cold.

Serves 4-6.

Sirloin with cream sauce

This dish is included in the lunch selection.

about 1,5 kg beef sirloin, fat and
  sinews removed
salt, black pepper and olive oil

CREAM SAUCE
250 ml (1 c) cream
5 ml (1 t) chicken stock powder
about 15-17 ml (3-3½ t) brandy
salt and pepper

Season the sirloin with salt and pepper and brush with a little olive oil. Braai the sirloin over hot coals for about 15 minutes a side, turning it only once. Wrap in aluminium foil to keep warm and slice into paper-thin slices just before serving.

Prepare the cream sauce by simmering the cream, stock powder and brandy together in a saucepan for about 10 minutes until the sauce has reduced and is slightly thickened. Season with salt and pepper to taste and pour over the sirloin slices.

Serves 8-10.

Springbok casserole

The onions provide enough moisture of their own, says Edwina, so it's not necessary to add any extra liquid. If, however, the dish looks too dry, you can add a little water.

olive oil
1 kg springbok shanks
2-3 onions, coarsely chopped
500 ml (2 c) red wine
1 chicken stock cube
30 ml (2 T) chopped fresh origanum
salt and freshly ground black pepper
500 g mushrooms, sliced
50 ml cream
50 ml chutney

Heat olive oil in a large heavy-based saucepan and lightly brown the shanks. Add the onions and sauté until tender and fragrant. Pour over the red wine and add the crumbled stock cube. Add the origanum and season generously with salt and freshly ground black pepper if necessary.

Bring to the boil, reduce the heat and cover. Simmer slowly for about 1½ hours, or until the meat is tender. Add the mushrooms and heat through.

Stir in the cream and chutney and simmer gently for about 1 minute. Transfer to a serving dish and serve hot.

Serves 6.

Fried potatoes

Kids in particular love potatoes done in this way.

5 large potatoes, peeled and cooked
1 onion, sliced
10 ml (2 t) olive oil

Slice the potatoes and set aside. Fry the onion in olive oil until tender, add the potato slices and fry with the onion until golden brown. Serve hot.

Serves 4-6.

Tongue with white wine mustard sauce

This sauce, flavoured with white wine, tastes completely different from ordinary mustard sauce.

WHITE WINE MUSTARD SAUCE

125 ml (½ c) white wine

125 ml (½ c) chicken stock

10 ml (2 t) Cape Country mustard

10 ml (2 t) white onion soup powder

salt and pepper (optional)

1 pickled tongue, cooked, and
  skin removed, thinly sliced

Heat the white wine and stock together in a saucepan and bring to the boil. Stir in the mustard and simmer gently.

Blend the onion soup powder with a little water to form a smooth paste and stir into the wine mixture. Simmer until the sauce comes to the boil and thickens slightly. Season to taste with salt and pepper if necessary and serve with the sliced tongue.

Serves 8-10.

Baked cheesecake with berry sauce

Cheesecake is always in demand, but served with this lovely berry sauce, which Edwina makes with the blackberries that grow around Swellendam, it's a real winner.

CRUST

half a 200-g packet Tennis biscuits, crushed

50 ml melted butter

FILLING

500 g (2 containers) creamed
   cottage cheese

180 ml (¾ c) castor sugar

3 extra-large eggs

75 ml (5 T) fresh lemon juice

250 ml (1 c) unwhipped cream

Preheat the oven to 155 °C (320 °F) and grease a 26-cm round loose-bottomed cake tin with butter or margarine or spray with nonstick spray.

Mix the crushed biscuits and butter and line the cake tin with the mixture. Chill until firm.

Mix the cottage cheese and castor sugar with a wooden spoon and add the eggs one by one, beating until well blended. Add the lemon juice. Fold in the cream and turn the filling into the prepared crust. Bake for 50 minutes and leave to cool at room temperature until set.

Makes 1 large cheesecake.

Berry sauce

500 g fresh or frozen blackberries
   or mixed berries

50 ml castor sugar

35 ml (7 t) port

Mix the berries and sugar together in a saucepan and simmer slowly for 30 minutes. Add the port, bring to the boil and remove from the heat. Cool and serve with the cheesecake.

The Orchard country and coffee shop in the Elgin area is a very popular stop along the N2. Here the traveller can enjoy a mouthwatering country breakfast or choose from a variety of light lunches and baked treats. The interesting, scrumptious open sandwiches, in particular, are worth trying. Everything is freshly prepared each day; even the cakes are baked daily at the coffee shop.

OPEN SANDWICHES

Whole-wheat bread with Creole char-grilled chicken

1 chicken breast fillet
salt
Creole spices (see recipe)
15 ml (1 T) oil
2 slices whole-wheat bread
shredded lettuce leaves
mayonnaise
a few slices tomato

CREOLE SPICES
5 ml (1 t) cayenne pepper
5 ml (1 t) white pepper
5 ml (1 t) black pepper
5 ml (1 t) dried thyme
5 ml (1 t) dried origanum
5 ml (1 t) brown sugar
15 ml (1 T) paprika
5 ml (1 t) crushed garlic

Place the chicken fillet between two layers of plastic wrap and flatten with the palm of your hand or with a meat mallet until about 2 mm thick and season lightly with salt. Mix all the ingredients for the Creole spices and spice the fillet generously on both sides.

Heat a pan until very hot, add the oil and heat until smoking. Grill the chicken fillet for about one minute on each side until charred.

Meanwhile, place the slices of bread on a plate. Moisten the lettuce with mayonnaise, place on top of the bread and top with a few tomato slices. Place the chicken fillet on top and serve immediately.

Serves 1.

Camembert and bacon bruschetta

You can't improve on the combination of flavours for this open sandwich.

2 slices bruschetta or French loaf,
    sliced diagonally
garlic butter (see recipe)
a few lettuce leaves
75 g mature Camembert cheese,
    sliced
3 rashers bacon, grilled
30 ml (2 T) apple jelly

Butter the bread on both sides with the garlic butter. Arrange on a baking sheet and grill under the oven grill until lightly browned.

Transfer the bread to a plate, top with a few lettuce leaves and arrange the cheese and bacon on top. Spoon over the apple jelly and serve immediately.

Serves 1.

Garlic butter

30 ml (2 T) butter
10 ml (2 t) crushed garlic
10 ml (2 t) chopped parsley
30 ml (2 T) olive oil
salt to taste

Blend all the ingredients and use as needed.

Health sandwich

A glass of freshly squeezed orange juice goes down well with this health sandwich.

handful sunflower seeds

oil

about 5 ml (1 t) soy sauce

2 slices whole-wheat bread

a few lettuce leaves

a few thin slices cucumber
   and tomato

a scoop of chunky cottage cheese

a few orange segments

paper-thin slices apple

a few bean sprouts

Fry the sunflower seeds in a little oil until lightly browned. Add the soy sauce and heat until most of the soy sauce has evaporated.

Place the whole-wheat bread on a plate and arrange the remaining ingredients on top. Sprinkle with the sunflower seeds.

Serves 1.

One of the Orchard's specialities is the wide selection of sumptuous cakes and other baked goodies. The Kahlua coffee cake and lemon and poppy seed cake are winners, while the delectable fruit tartlets taste as good as they look.

Lemon and poppy seed cake

250 g butter

350 ml castor sugar

3 extra-large eggs

grated rind of 2 lemons

450 ml cake flour

10 ml (2 t) baking powder

2 ml (½ t) salt

60 ml (¼ c) water

45 ml (3 T) lemon juice

80 ml (⅓ c) poppy seeds

SYRUP

250 ml (1 c) sugar

125 ml (½ c) water

125 ml (½ c) lemon juice

ICING

110 g butter

700 ml icing sugar

100 g smooth cream cheese

extra poppy seeds

candied lemon peel strips
   (optional)

Preheat the oven to 190 °C (375 °F). Grease a 24-cm springform cake tin well with butter or margarine or spray with nonstick spray.

Whisk the butter and sugar together until light and creamy. Add the eggs one by one, beating well after each addition. Add the lemon rind. Sift the flour, baking powder and salt together twice. Mix the water and lemon juice. Fold the flour mixture into the butter mixture, alternating with the water mixture. Add the poppy seeds and mix. Turn into the prepared tin and bake for about 35-45 minutes or until a skewer comes out clean when inserted into the centre of the cake.

Meanwhile, heat the sugar, water and lemon juice for the syrup until the sugar has dissolved. Bring to the boil. Pour over the warm cake and leave to cool in the tin.

Cream the butter until light and fluffy. Add the icing sugar little by little, beating well. Beat in the cream cheese. Turn the cake out onto a serving platter, spoon the icing on top, sprinkle with poppy seeds and decorate with candied lemon peel strips, if preferred.

Makes a medium-sized cake.

Kahlua coffee cake

This cake has to be chilled overnight to become firm.

CAKE

6 extra-large eggs, separated

680 ml (2¾ c) castor sugar

680 ml (2¾ c) cake flour

30 ml (2 T) baking powder

45 ml (3 T) cocoa

45 ml (3 T) butter

375 ml (1½ c) milk

SYRUP

125 ml (½ c) sugar

125 ml (½ c) water

30 ml (2 T) Kahlua liqueur

FILLING

200 ml milk

100 ml sugar

10 ml (2 t) instant coffee
   granules

3 extra-large eggs, separated

10 ml (2 t) gelatine sprinkled over
   30 ml (2 T) cold water

60 ml (4 T) Kahlua liqueur

500 ml (2 c) cream, chilled

ICING

10 ml (2 t) gelatine

40 ml (8 t) cold water

500 ml (2 c) cream, chilled

60 ml (¼ c) castor sugar

Preheat the oven to 180 °C (350 °F). Grease a large 30-cm springform cake tin with butter or margarine or spray with nonstick spray. Line the sides with baking paper.

Whisk the egg whites until stiff but not dry. Gradually whisk in the sugar, add the egg yolks and whisk until pale and light.

Sift the flour, baking powder and cocoa together twice. Boil the butter and milk together. Fold the flour mixture into the egg mixture, alternating with the milk mixture. Turn into the prepared tin and bake for about 70 minutes or until a skewer comes out clean when inserted into the centre of the cake. Leave the cake to cool slightly in the tin before turning out onto a wire rack to cool completely. Cut the cake into three layers horizontally.

Meanwhile, prepare the syrup: Heat the sugar and water until the sugar has dissolved. Bring to the boil and boil for about 5 minutes or until syrupy. Remove from the heat, add the liqueur and cool completely. Spoon over each of the cake layers.

Prepare the filling: Boil the milk, sugar and coffee together. Whisk the egg yolks until light and add the hot milk mixture while beating continuously. Heat over boiling water while beating continuously until the mixture thickens slightly, but does not come to the boil. Add the gelatine and liqueur and mix. Cool completely. Whip the cream until stiff and beat the egg whites until stiff peaks form. Fold both the cream and egg whites into the cooled coffee mixture.

Line the cake tin with baking paper once again. Place a cake layer in the bottom of the cake tin, followed by a layer of filling. Repeat, ending with a cake layer. Cool overnight. Unmould the cake onto a cake platter.

Prepare the icing: Mix the gelatine with the cold water and leave for 5 minutes. Melt in the microwave oven, but do not bring to the boil. Whip the cream until stiff, whisk in the castor sugar and fold in the melted gelatine. Cover the top and sides of the cake with the icing and decorate with cream rosettes.

Makes 1 large cake.

Kahlua coffee cake (left) and lemon and poppy seed cake (right), p. 155

Fruit tartlets

PASTRY

5 x 250 ml (5 c) cake flour

pinch salt

pinch sugar

500 g cold margarine

about 250 ml (1 c) ice-cold water

250 g white chocolate

CUSTARD FILLING

1 litre (4 c) milk

250 ml (1 c) sugar

200 ml custard powder

5 ml (1 t) vanilla essence

20 ml (4 t) gelatine

30 ml (2 T) cold water

250 ml (1 c) cream, stiffly whipped

TOPPING

variety of fresh fruit such as melon balls,
   fresh pineapple, blueberries,
   raspberries or grapes

GLAZE

125 ml (½ c) water

5 ml (1 t) lemon juice

60 ml (¼ c) sugar

3 ml (generous ½ t) gelatine

Grease a few tartlet tins (8 cm in diameter) well with butter or margarine or spray with nonstick spray.

Sift the cake flour, salt and sugar together. Grate in the margarine and rub in with your fingertips until well blended and the mixture resembles breadcrumbs. Add enough ice-cold water to form a stiff dough that is easy to roll out. Shape into a ball, cover with plastic wrap and chill for about 20 minutes. Roll out on a lightly floured surface until about 2 mm thick. Cut out circles slightly larger than the tartlet tins. Line the tins with the pastry circles and chill once more for about 20 minutes. Trim the edges. Line each of the tartlets with baking paper and fill with dried beans.

Preheat the oven to 190 °C (375 °F) and bake for 10 minutes. Remove the baking paper and beans and bake for another 10 minutes. Cool, melt the white chocolate and brush each of the crusts with the melted chocolate.

Mix 250 ml (1 c) of the milk with the sugar and custard powder. Bring the remaining milk to the boil. Blend in the custard powder mixture and bring to the boil while stirring continuously. Add the vanilla essence. Cool completely until ice cold.

Soak the gelatine in the cold water until spongy. Heat until dissolved but do not allow to boil. Place the cold custard in the food processor and process while slowly adding the melted gelatine. Fold in the cream. Turn into the prepared crusts and decorate with fruit as preferred.

Mix all the ingredients for the glaze and leave for 5 minutes. Microwave until the gelatine has melted but do not allow to boil. Cool until firm, but not set. Coat the tartlets with the glaze.

Makes about 50 tartlets.

Valley of elephants, citrus and roses

Addo, Sunland, Summerville – important-sounding names for tiny Eastern Cape villages in the Sundays River valley. Together they form a patchwork of citrus orchards, each hemmed with windbreaks. The Addo Elephant National Park, home to about three hundred elephant, is also found here. The name Addo derives from the Khoikhoi word "kardouw", meaning "river path". While driving through the valley, however, I remember thinking that a name like "Valley of Plenty" is much more appropriate . . . apart from citrus and elephants, Addo is also famous for its huge rose show – and there are many game farms and horse studs in the area. On Sundays, they play polo at the club.

The Sundays River valley is gearing up for an increasing number of visitors. A short while ago, there was only one bed and breakfast establishment, now there are eighteen. You can camp out in log cabins on the riverbanks, relax on a working citrus farm or treat yourself to colonial-style luxury. During our whirlwind visit in August 2000 it was impossible to explore the area thoroughly, but the hospitality we were shown, the temperate climate and, above all, the expansion of the Addo Elephant National Park to accommodate more animals, convinced us that this was going to become the ideal holiday destination – a refuge from the wet Cape winter.

The annual citrus festival brought us to Sunland. At the Sundays River Primary School an enormous picture had been made, using citrus. There were stalls and drum majorettes, and even a special train transporting visitors from Port Elizabeth.

Arriving at Woodhall at dusk, we immediately saw why this bed and breakfast guesthouse had been nominated by the AA as the best farm accommodation in the country for three consecutive years. We enjoyed sundowners in the beautiful garden, with its wooden deck overlooking the farm dam where swans glided gracefully, and we feasted on pittas and sweet potato bread, salmon and sun-dried tomato spreads, and olive tapenade.

The Elephant House is situated at the junction on the way to the Addo Elephant National Park. At night lanterns are lit around the thatched homestead. Everything speaks of stylish, elegant simplicity – the heavy wooden swing doors, overhanging thatched roofs and rough-plastered walls around the open courtyard. Leather and old Cape furniture are grouped tastefully on the porch, where guests also have their meals. When it's cold, the huge blinds are pulled down to make the area warm and cosy.

Also close to the Addo Elephant National Park is a crocodile farm where you can show your children crocodiles of all sizes, as well as a tame camel, lions and wolves. It also boasts a restaurant, The Lair, where rare items such as blue wildebeest steaks and crocodile meat appear on the menu.

Cosmos Cuisine could be considered Sunland's beacon, because it's more or less on the boundary of the town. In the cosy dining room of this guesthouse next to the railway line you can enjoy breakfast, lunch or dinner prepared by Elsona Deetlefs, a well-known caterer in the area.

Woodhall is a working citrus farm which has been in the Miller family for generations. At first, James and Debbie Miller had only one room for overnight guests, who also ate at the family table. Soon, however, they had to expand the facilities to a fully fledged bed and breakfast guesthouse. Here, with the help of their cousin, Margie Tarr, they prepare and serve food with single-minded devotion.

Crisp pitta breads

These crunchy pitta breads are ideal for serving with spreads.

1,5 kg white bread flour

15 ml (1 T) salt

1½ packets instant yeast

2 extra-large eggs

600 ml milk

300 ml water

60 ml (¼ c) butter, melted

dried herbs such as rosemary, marjoram and origanum

coarse salt and freshly ground black pepper to taste

Preheat the oven to 220 °C (425 °F) and grease a baking sheet with butter or margarine or spray with nonstick spray.

Combine the flour and salt. Sprinkle the yeast on top and make a well in the centre. Beat the eggs, milk and water together and add to the flour mixture. Mix into a dough. On a floured surface, knead the dough until smooth and elastic and no longer sticking to your hands. Cover with a damp cloth and leave to rise in a warm place until doubled in volume.

Knock the dough back and knead again. Break off pieces of the dough and roll out into thin circles with a rolling pin. Brush with melted butter and sprinkle with herbs, salt and pepper.

Bake for 5-7 minutes until pale brown and crisp. (Alternatively, bake the bread until just done, brush with oil and grill in the oven until pale brown.) Break into chunks and serve with spreads.

Makes about 35 pittas.

Sweet potato loaf

The recipe for this wonderfully crisp bread comes from a Portuguese friend of her mom, says Debbie.

500 g cooked sweet potato, mashed

900 ml lukewarm water

1,5 kg cake flour

20 ml (4 t) salt

1½ packets instant yeast

Preheat the oven to 220 °C (425 °F) and grease 2 baking sheets with butter or margarine or spray with nonstick spray.

Blend the sweet potato and lukewarm water until smooth and set aside.

Place the cake flour, salt and instant yeast in a large mixing bowl and make a well in the centre. Add the sweet potato mixture and mix to form a dough. Knead the dough well on a floured surface until smooth and elastic and until it no longer sticks to your hands, cover with a cloth and leave to rise in a warm place until doubled in volume.

Knock the dough back and divide into four uniform pieces. Shape each piece into a slightly flattened ball and place two balls on each of the baking sheets, leaving sufficient room in between for rising. Leave to rise once more in a warm place.

Dust with cake flour and bake for 15 minutes. Reduce the oven temperature to 190 °C (375 °F) and bake for another 30-40 minutes until golden brown and done.

Makes 4 medium-sized loaves.

Sun-dried tomato spread

90 g sun-dried tomatoes
500 ml (2 c) water
30 ml (2 T) olive oil
2 cloves garlic, crushed
5 ml (1 t) finely grated lemon rind
5 ml (1 t) dried basil
3 ml (generous ½ t) freshly ground black pepper
60 ml (¼ c) olives, stoned and finely chopped
15 ml (1 T) capers, drained

Heat the sun-dried tomatoes and water in a small saucepan and bring to the boil. Cover, reduce the heat and simmer for about 10 minutes or until the tomatoes are completely soft. Drain well and pat dry with paper towelling.

Place all the ingredients in a food processor and process gently until the ingredients are well blended but the mixture is still fairly coarse.

Makes 375 ml (1½ c) spread.

Smoked salmon spread

180 g smoked salmon
15 ml (1 T) lemon juice
pinch freshly ground black pepper
60 ml (¼ c) mayonnaise
250 g (1 container) creamed cottage cheese
5 ml (1 t) dried dill
lemon wedges and sprigs of dill to garnish

Cut the salmon into small pieces with kitchen scissors. Sprinkle with lemon juice and black pepper. Add the mayonnaise, creamed cottage cheese and dill and mix well with a wooden spoon. Chill for two hours, garnish with lemon wedges and fresh sprigs of dill and serve.

Makes 375 ml (1½ c) spread.

Olive tapenade

1 tin (50 g) anchovy fillets
250 ml (1 c) calamata olives, stoned
   and finely chopped
60 ml (¼ c) capers, coarsely chopped
60 ml (¼ c) finely chopped fresh parsley
45 ml (3 T) finely chopped fresh basil
2 cloves garlic, crushed
15 ml (1 T) prepared mustard
15 ml (1 T) lemon juice
125 ml (½ c) olive oil

Place all the ingredients in a food processor and process until smooth.

Makes 250 ml (1 c) tapenade.

A variety of snacks including sun-dried tomato spread (below left), olive tapenade (below), crisp pitta breads (right), p. 163, and sweet potato loaf (far right), p. 163

Initially all they intended starting was a horse stud, says Ann Read of The Elephant House. The place was bushy and overgrown. One day, standing among the bushes and listening to all the cars driving past to the elephant park, she suddenly realised that a guesthouse would be the answer. Ann says she prefers simple country flavours to fancy, elaborate dishes. This dessert, which she made specially for us, is one of her favourites.

Pears in white wine

60 ml (¼ c) honey

30 ml (2 T) brown sugar

2 cinnamon sticks

350 ml semi-sweet white wine

15 ml (1 T) grated fresh orange rind

4 pears, peeled, but keep the stems intact

Place all the ingredients, except the pears, in a saucepan and cover. Heat slowly over low heat until the sugar has melted.

Bring to the boil, add the pears and simmer gently for about 30-35 minutes or until the pears are soft enough to be cut with a spoon. Cool the pears in the poaching liquid and serve with cream if desired.

Serves 2-4.

Elsona Deetlefs of Cosmos Cuisine is well known in the area for her catering skills, especially for her sumptuous food and baked goods. It was actually a hobby that turned into a career, she says.

Giant breakfast scones

Served with marmalade and freshly squeezed orange juice these scones are delicious for breakfast. Elsona bakes them in deep muffin pans so they're uniform in size.

125 ml (½ c) oil
1 extra-large egg, whisked
milk
20 ml (4 t) lemon juice
500 ml (2 c) cake flour
20 ml (4 t) baking powder
25 ml (5 t) sugar
3 ml (generous ½ t) salt

Preheat the oven to 190 °C (375 °F) and grease the hollows of a muffin pan with butter or margarine or spray with nonstick spray.

Blend the oil and egg and add enough milk to make up 250 ml (1 c) liquid. Add the lemon juice. Sift the dry ingredients together and make a well in the centre. Add the milk mixture and mix lightly with a spatula until just blended. (The mixture is fairly stiff.)

Spoon the batter into the hollows of the muffin pan and bake for about 15-20 minutes or until done and nicely risen.

Makes 9 scones.

Stir-fried calamari

The calamari is served with a flavoursome coarse tomato and sweet pepper sauce, making it strikingly different from the usual versions.

½ green sweet pepper, seeded
   and chopped
1 medium onion, finely chopped
1 clove garlic, crushed
olive oil
1 tomato, peeled and finely chopped
2 mushrooms, sliced
3-4 calamari steaks, cut into strips
5 ml (1 t) lemon juice
salt and freshly ground black pepper
   to taste

Sauté the sweet pepper, onion and garlic in olive oil until tender. Add the tomato and stir-fry lightly. Add the mushrooms and stir-fry. Set the tomato mixture aside, keeping it warm.

Rapidly fry the calamari strips in a little heated oil until just done, taking care not to overcook it as it will become tough. Season with lemon juice and salt and freshly ground black pepper to taste. Stir in the tomato sauce and serve with rice.

Serves 2.

Smoked springbok salad

The salad dressing, made with orange juice, goes beautifully with the springbok.

1 packet (150 g) smoked springbok slices
    or moist beef biltong, thinly sliced
a variety of fresh salad greens such as
    rocket, and mustard and butter lettuce
fresh basil and fennel
a few plump raisins

SALAD DRESSING
200 ml olive oil
20 ml (4 t) orange juice
5 ml (1 t) Tabasco sauce

Arrange the meat on a salad platter along with the salad greens, basil and fennel. Scatter the raisins on top.

Blend the ingredients for the salad dressing and sprinkle over the salad.

Serves 2-4.

Chicken rolls with wine and cheese sauce

The wine and cheese sauce is the perfect accompaniment to the juicy chicken rolls.

1 lemon

1 clove garlic, crushed

200 ml butter, melted

4 boned chicken breasts, skinned

salt and freshly ground black pepper
   to taste

4 slices ham

4 fingers Cheddar cheese

1 extra-large egg, whisked

200 ml fresh breadcrumbs

oil

WINE AND CHEESE SAUCE

250 ml (1 c) thick white sauce

200 ml grated Cheddar cheese

25 ml (5 t) dry white wine

Finely grate the lemon rind and squeeze out the lemon juice. Blend the lemon juice and rind with the garlic and melted butter and set aside.

Flatten the chicken breasts slightly with a meat mallet and brush with the lemon and garlic butter. Season lightly with salt and black pepper. Place a slice of ham and a cheese finger on each chicken breast and carefully roll it up. Secure with string or cocktail sticks. Roll the chicken breasts in the whisked egg and then in the breadcrumbs. Chill for about 15 minutes.

Heat the oil and fry the chicken rolls until golden brown. Cover, reduce the heat slightly and steam the chicken rolls until done.

Heat the white sauce and stir in the cheese and white wine. Serve the chicken rolls with the hot wine and cheese sauce and a yellow rice timbale into which a little chopped sweet pepper, onions and mushrooms have been mixed.

Serves 4.

Batter bread

A quick and delicious batter bread.

500 ml (2 c) cake flour
500 ml (2 c) whole-wheat flour
500 ml (2 c) milk
60 ml (¼ c) brown sugar
7 ml (1½ t) bicarbonate of soda
15 ml (1 T) salt
10 ml (2 t) lemon juice
poppy and sunflower seeds
   for sprinkling on top

Preheat the oven to 190 °C (375 °F) and grease a large loaf tin well with butter or margarine or spray with nonstick spray.

Mix all the ingredients, except the seeds, and turn into the prepared loaf tin. Sprinkle the seeds on top and bake for about an hour or until a skewer comes out clean when inserted into the centre of the bread.

Makes 1 medium-sized loaf.

Banana and caramel cheesecake

When you taste this unbaked cheesecake you immediately assume the recipe must be complicated, but it's actually very easy. Fabian Marais, who occasionally helps out at Cosmos Cuisine, prefers this cheesecake – and it's sheer temptation! As it contains no gelatine, chill the cake overnight to ensure that the filling is firm, although still soft and creamy.

CRUST
1½ packets (200 g each) Tennis
   biscuits, crushed
150 g butter, melted

FILLING
250 ml (1 c) cream, chilled
60 ml (¼ c) castor sugar
2-3 containers (each 250 g)
   cream cheese or creamed
   cottage cheese
1 tin (375 g) caramel condensed
   milk
3 large ripe bananas
cocoa for sifting on top

Grease a 25-cm loose-bottomed cake tin with butter or margarine or spray with nonstick spray. Line the base and sides with aluminium foil. Butter well or spray the foil with nonstick spray.

Mix the biscuit crumbs and melted butter together and press into the base and halfway along the sides of the tin.

Whip the cream and castor sugar together until stiff and fold in the cream cheese or cottage cheese. Chill the mixture until stiff. Spread the caramel condensed milk over the biscuit base. Slice the bananas and arrange on the caramel layer. Pour the cream cheese mixture into the crust and dust with cocoa. Chill, preferably overnight, until firm. Serve with tea or as a dessert. Keep chilled.

Makes 1 large cheesecake.

Banana and caramel cheesecake

Truffles

As they depart, each guest is presented with one of these truffels. It's hard to believe that these delectable truffles are made from oats and biscuits.

300 ml milk

200 g butter

125 ml (½ c) castor sugar

125 ml (½ c) cocoa powder

200 ml oats

1 packet (300 g) digestive biscuits, crushed

40 ml (8 t) rum essence

melted chocolate

Heat the milk, butter, castor sugar and cocoa over low heat until the castor sugar has dissolved. Stir occasionally. Bring to the boil and simmer for 5 minutes.

Add the oats and simmer for about 3 minutes until thick and cooked. Cool until lukewarm and stir in the biscuit crumbs and rum essence. Cool to room temperature, roll into balls and place in the fridge to firm.

Drizzle with melted chocolate or dip into the melted chocolate and chill until needed.

Makes 50 truffles.

It's thanks to young Marius Botha's Italian and French cooking background that the food at the restaurant on the crocodile farm is so well prepared. I was particularly impressed by the interesting flavour and texture combinations; I even tried a morsel of crocodile meat. The meat has no particular flavour – the crisp onion rings, coated in masala, made the dish special.

Coarse tomato salsa

At The Lair this sauce is served with the crocodile meat, but it goes equally well with pan-fried chicken or fish.

50 ml tomato sauce

50 ml apricot jam

70 ml (4 T + 2 t) chutney

10 ml (2 t) soy sauce

15 ml (1 T) white vinegar

50 ml olive oil

1 large onion, sliced into thick rings

5 ml (1 t) masala

1-2 tomatoes, skinned and coarsely
   chopped

Place the tomato sauce, jam, chutney, soy sauce, vinegar and olive oil in a food processor and process until smooth. Pour into a saucepan and bring to the boil.

Meanwhile, heat a little olive oil in a large pan. Rapidly fry the onion rings for a few seconds until glossy but still crisp. Add the masala, stir-fry for a few seconds and then stir in the cooked sauce. Finally add the chopped tomato and heat through until just warm, not cooked. Spoon over fried chicken or fish portions.

Makes 500 ml (2 c) sauce.

Coarse tomato salsa

Festive fare in
Kannaland

Nowadays it's called the Little Karoo, but in days gone by it was known as Kannaland – and what better name for this beautiful region caught between the Swartberg Mountains on one side and the towering Outeniquas on the other? In spring the veld is ablaze with red aloes in full bloom, and dusky pink Chinese lanterns grow in abundance at the roadside – here, too, you will see herds of ostrich grazing in the veld.

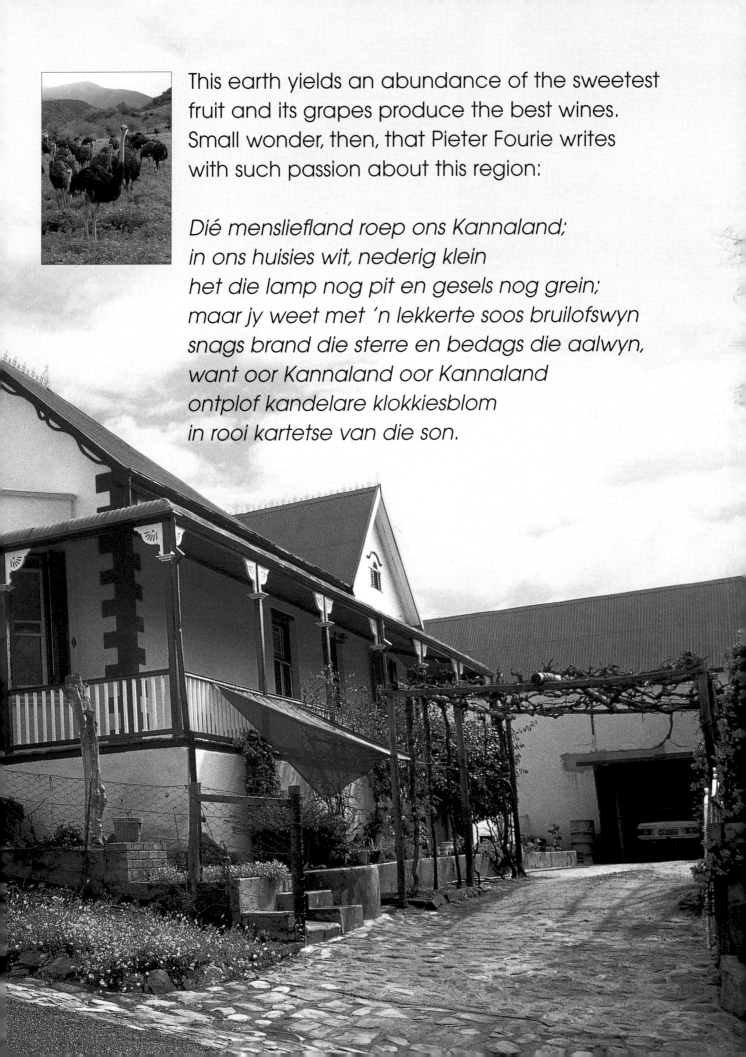

This earth yields an abundance of the sweetest
fruit and its grapes produce the best wines.
Small wonder, then, that Pieter Fourie writes
with such passion about this region:

Dié mensliefland roep ons Kannaland;
in ons huisies wit, nederig klein
het die lamp nog pit en gesels nog grein;
maar jy weet met 'n lekkerte soos bruilofswyn
snags brand die sterre en bedags die aalwyn,
want oor Kannaland oor Kannaland
ontplof kandelare klokkiesblom
in rooi kartetse van die son.

In the spring of '94, *You* travelled to the Little Karoo for the first time. We visited Calitzdorp, the port capital, and De Rust, that quaint Victorian hamlet from the previous century nestling in the foothills of the Great Swartberg Mountains. At that time the festival was no more than rumour, but one could sense that something momentous was about to happen. I remember, one Saturday morning, visiting Jans Rautenbach – the current chairman of the Little Karoo National Arts Festival – at his stone house. He waxed lyrical about the beauty of the region and could not stop talking about an Afrikaans festival they were planning, which would be a first.

In 2000 we went there again, this time to attend the festival at Oudtshoorn – which was bursting at the seams – and to indulge in roosterkoek and sosaties, braai chops and sausages, ribs, koeksisters and strong coffee. We were also introduced to the Karoo hamburger: roosterkoek sandwiching a boned chop! The festival had its own shebeen, offering meat, samp and pumpkin dished up from black cast-iron pots. But the established eateries in Oudtshoorn provided the surprises on the gourmet menu.

Jemima's is the restaurant belonging to the Le Roux sisters, Annette and Celia. During the festival they offer a special festive menu consisting of delectable boerekos with a Mediterranean flavour, mainly because the Little Karoo climate resembles that of the Mediterranean region. From their parents' farm, Doornkraal, about 40 km from Oudtshoorn, they get products such as rocket salad and fresh herbs, habanero chillies, wonderful jams and quince jelly, elephant garlic, fresh green asparagus and flowering courgettes.

Annette says her mother, Ann, is her great inspiration. They're a large family of seven children and are used to convivial meals at the farm. Even though they have not travelled much, their parents have, says Annette, and it's a privilege to sample all their mother's experiments.

Voorbroodjies with chickpea spread

One of Jemima's tasty offerings is a griddlecake. They call it a voorbroodjie and serve it with a spread. They use a full-cream cottage cheese as a base for the spread and add whatever takes their fancy – paprika, brinjals or olives. The chickpea spread is very popular and easy to make. The restaurant uses tinned chickpeas but dried ones can be used if you prefer them, provided you soak them overnight and boil them until soft.

1 tin (410 g) chickpeas, drained
15 ml (1 T) tahini (sesame seed paste)
juice of 1 lemon
2 cloves garlic, crushed
45 ml (3 T) finely chopped Italian parsley
10 ml (2 t) chopped fresh mint leaves
salt and freshly ground black pepper to taste
125 ml (½ c) olive oil
250 ml (1 c) cream cheese

Process all the ingredients except the olive oil and cream cheese in a blender until smooth, drizzling in the olive oil in a steady stream. Add the cream cheese and stir through until well mixed and smooth.

Makes about 600 ml.

Brinjal spread

Use the same recipe and ingredients but use two medium brinjals instead of the chickpeas. Slice the brinjals lengthwise and place the halves (skin side up) on a baking sheet greased with about 30 ml (2 T) olive oil. Bake until the brinjals are soft. Cool and process in a blender until smooth.

The festive table featured choice salads. "Our salads are all easy to make," says Annette. "And they're all old favourites seasoned imaginatively."

Green bean salad

The fried sunflower seeds make this an outstanding salad.

about 500 g young green beans, topped and tailed
125 ml (½ c) sunflower seeds
15 ml (1 T) oil
125 ml (½ c) soy sauce

Blanch the beans for a few minutes in boiling salted water and refresh them in ice-cold water. Fry the sunflower seeds lightly in the oil until just golden (be careful, as they burn easily). Add the soy sauce (careful, it may splatter) and pour the sauce over the beans.
Serves 6.

Tomato salad

4-6 very ripe tomatoes, cut into wedges
1 onion, sliced into rings

DRESSING
125 ml (½ c) red wine vinegar
125 ml (½ c) sunflower oil
125 ml (½ c) olive oil
salt and freshly ground black pepper to taste

Arrange the tomatoes and onions in a glass bowl.
Beat all the dressing ingredients together, season with salt and pepper and sprinkle over the salad.
Serves 6-8.

Tomato salad

Lamb shanks in muscadel sauce

Annette says her mom cooks this dish overnight in the oven of her Aga stove instead of in a saucepan.

6 whole lamb shanks

salt and freshly ground black pepper

butter and olive oil

4 onions, peeled and cubed

4 celery stalks, chopped with leaves
    and all

4 carrots, peeled and cubed

30 ml (2 T) butter

1 large tin (115 g) tomato paste

6 cloves garlic, peeled

2 bay leaves

a sprig of fresh rosemary and thyme

250 ml (1 c) red wine

750 ml (1 bottle) muscadel

hot water

1 tin (400 g) whole, peeled tomatoes

Wash the shanks, season with salt and pepper and brown in a little heated butter and olive oil. Remove from the pan and set aside. Sauté the onions, celery and carrots in 30 ml (2 T) butter in a large saucepan until glazed. Add the shanks and tomato paste. Simmer for about a minute and add the garlic and herbs. Add the red wine and cook through. Add half the muscadel and just enough hot water to cover the meat and vegetables. Reduce the heat and simmer for at least 1 hour, or until the meat is tender. Carefully remove the shanks. Now add the peeled tomatoes and the rest of the muscadel. Reduce the sauce until thick and flavoursome. You can also thicken it by bringing it to the boil while adding a paste of cake flour and a little water.

Season with salt and freshly ground black pepper and serve with polenta (p. 181), if preferred.

Serves 6.

Steve Grobler's "smoky ribs"

These ribs are extremely popular. Steve Grobler, their butcher, marinates the ribs for them in his special sauce, ready for oven-roasting or braaiing without any further ado.

MARINADE
500 ml (2 c) hot water
125 ml (½ c) tomato purée
125 ml (½ c) apple purée
125 ml (½ c) soy sauce
60 ml (¼ c) brown sugar
60 ml (¼ c) honey
7 ml (1½ t) salt
3 ml (generous ½ t) ground
   black pepper
3 ml (generous ½ t) ground
   ginger
375 ml (1½ c) sunflower oil

1 rack of lamb, sliced into ribs

Mix the ingredients for the marinade and set aside to cool. Place the ribs in the marinade and leave overnight.

Preheat the oven to 170 °C (340 °F). Arrange the ribs in a roasting pan and roast in the oven or braai over medium coals until done and the fat is well cooked. Take care not to overcook – they'll be too dry.

Serves 4-6.

Van der Hum bread and butter pudding

This delicious pudding earned full marks in our test kitchen.

125 ml (½ c) fruitcake mix

125 ml (½ c) Van der Hum liqueur

1 day-old loaf raisin bread

100 ml soft butter

apricot jam (optional)

300 ml cream

300 ml milk

5 ml (1 t) vanilla essence

8 extra-large egg yolks

200 ml white sugar

60 ml (¼ c) caramel brown sugar

Preheat the oven to 180 °C (350 °F) and grease a 27-cm oven-proof dish with butter or margarine or spray with nonstick spray.

Place the fruitcake mix in a bowl and cover with the liqueur. Leave in a warm place or heat slightly in the microwave oven. Remove the crusts of the raisin bread, slice thickly and spread both sides of each slice with butter. (You can also spread one side with apricot jam.) Cut into triangles and arrange in a single layer on the base of the dish. Sprinkle the fruit and liqueur mixture over the bread and cover with a second layer of bread.

Heat the cream and milk until almost boiling. Add the vanilla essence. Beat the egg yolks and sugar until light and thick and slowly add the milk mixture, stirring well to blend. Pour over the pudding and bake for about 40 minutes. The pudding will rise like a soufflé and sink again.

Remove from the oven, sprinkle with caramel brown sugar and place immediately under a heated grill.

Serve with ice cream or cream.

Serves 8-10.

In 1994 we visited Swepie and Ann le Roux at their farm, Domein Doornkraal outside De Rust, where they produce a wide variety of excellent wines. Ann is renowned for preparing "food with a difference", and her passion for honest, tasty food has been handed on to her children. Nowadays she serves as inspiration to her daughters Annette and Celia, owners of the restaurant Jemima's in Oudtshoorn. Her food stall has also been honoured as the best at the arts festival.

Portuguese tartlets

These tartlets resemble milk tart.

1 roll (400 g) puff pastry or phyllo
   pastry to line the pans

4 egg yolks

250 ml (1 c) creamy milk

150 ml sugar

5 ml (1 t) ground cinnamon

pinch salt

Preheat the oven to 180 °C (350 °F). Grease medium muffin pans (not for large muffins) with butter. Line the muffin hollows with the puff pastry or 4 layers of phyllo pastry, remembering first to brush each layer of phyllo pastry with butter.

Beat the remaining ingredients together and pour into the lined hollows of the muffin pans. Bake for 20-30 minutes until the filling for the tartlets has set and is golden brown on top. Sprinkle with extra cinnamon once the tartlets have been removed from the oven.

Makes 20-30 tartlets.

Kefta

The pungent flavours of this Mediterranean dish go well with the Kannaland climate, says Ann. Make it well in advance to allow the flavours to blend, and reheat just before serving. Serve with rice, couscous or even crumbly porridge.

750 g minced mutton (with a little fat)

½ medium onion, finely chopped

a few mint leaves, finely chopped

a few sprigs parsley, finely chopped

a little marjoram, fresh or dried

salt and freshly ground black pepper to taste

2 ml (½ t) cayenne pepper

2 ml (½ t) ground cumin

2 ml (½ t) paprika

1 ml (¼ t) of two or more of the following: nutmeg, ground cinnamon, ground cloves, ground ginger or cardamom seeds

butter for frying

SAUCE

1 large onion, finely chopped

1 clove garlic, crushed

250 ml (1 c) of any one or all of the following: brinjal, sweet pepper, courgettes, thinly sliced

60 ml (4 T) olive oil

500 g ripe red tomatoes, skinned and coarsely chopped

250 ml (1 c) water

paprika or cayenne pepper

5 ml (1 t) apricot jam

salt

30 ml (2 T) finely chopped parsley

Mix the mince, onion and seasonings, adding more seasonings if necessary as the flavour should be fairly sharp, says Ann. Wet your hands and shape the mixture into small meatballs.

In a shallow saucepan, bring a little water to the boil and poach the meatballs for 10 minutes. Drain and fry the meatballs in a little melted butter until golden brown.

Sauté the onion, garlic and vegetables in the olive oil for a few minutes to allow the flavours to emerge. Add the tomatoes and water and simmer for about an hour until the sauce is fairly smooth and thick. Season to taste with paprika or cayenne pepper, and add the apricot jam and salt to taste. Transfer the meatballs to the saucepan with the sauce and simmer for at least 10 minutes. Sprinkle with parsley.

Serves 4-6.

Turkey potpies

Ann keeps a few turkeys on the farm and says she prefers turkey to chicken. Turkey is now readily available in most supermarkets.

2 kg turkey pieces
1 litre (4 c) water
2 chicken stock cubes
250 ml (1 c) white wine
1 carrot, scraped and coarsely chopped
1 celery stalk, coarsely chopped
1 onion, coarsely chopped
few sprigs parsley
1 bay leaf
8 peppercorns
500 ml (2 c) finely chopped carrot
125 g button mushrooms, quartered
500 ml (2 c) finely chopped leeks
250 ml (1 c) finely chopped celery
250 ml (1 c) finely chopped sweet pepper
150 ml butter
250 ml (1 c) thick cream
75 ml (5 T) cake flour
15 ml (1 T) lemon juice
salt and freshly ground black pepper
  to taste
1 packet (400 g) frozen puff pastry, thawed
egg yolk and water for brushing on top

Place the turkey pieces, water, chicken stock cubes and wine in a saucepan and add the carrot, celery, onion, parsley, bay leaf and peppercorns. Simmer until the meat is tender, remove it from the liquid and cool. Skin and bone the meat and return the skin and bones to the stock. Cube the meat. Slowly simmer the stock with the skin and bones for another hour, strain through a fine sieve and measure off 3½ cups.

Sauté the carrots, mushrooms, leeks, celery and sweet pepper in half the butter until tender. Add half a cup of the measured stock and simmer slowly until the stock has reduced.

Add the cream and remaining stock to a saucepan and simmer slowly. Melt the remaining butter in a pan, stir in the cake flour and then quickly stir the flour mixture into the cream mixture. Stir until smooth and until the cream mixture thickens. Remove from the heat and stir in the lemon juice. Add the cubed turkey and the sautéed vegetables and mix. Season to taste with salt and pepper. Spoon the mixture into six 2-cup ovenproof dishes, or into one large ovenproof dish. Leave to cool.

Roll out the puff pastry until thinner and cut out six circles to fit on top of the dishes. Brush the edges of each dish with the egg yolk mixture, place the pastry circles on top and brush each pastry circle with the egg mixture. Bake at 200 °C (400 °F) for about 20-30 minutes or until the puff pastry is golden brown on top.

Makes 6 large portions.

It was a spur-of-the-moment decision to buy De Fijne Keuken Restaurant in Oudtshoorn, says owner Susan Lategan. It took them a mere four days to pull down walls, paint the restaurant, compile menus and buy the ingredients needed. Then they invited friends and acquaintances to the opening – and learnt to cook as the orders came in!

Chicken pittas

500 g chicken breast fillets, skinned,
  boned and cut into strips
olive oil
1 clove garlic, crushed
2-cm piece fresh ginger, finely grated
250-300 ml sweet-and-sour sauce
  (preferably Kikkoman)
100 ml water
15 ml (1 T) Worcester sauce
honey to taste
salt and freshly ground black pepper to taste
5 pitta breads, slit open

Fry the chicken strips in a little olive oil until browned. Add the garlic and ginger. Lightly stir-fry, then add the sweet-and-sour sauce, water, Worcester sauce and honey. Bring to the boil and simmer until the sauce has reduced slightly. Season to taste with salt and pepper. Spoon the mixture into the pitta breads.

Serves 5.

Spinakopitas

You's editorial team really loved this one.

600 g (2 packets) spinach

2 onions, finely chopped

2 cloves garlic, crushed

olive oil

salt and freshly ground black pepper
  to taste

pinch nutmeg

pinch origanum

250 ml (1 c) crumbled feta cheese

400 g (1 packet) phyllo pastry

100 g (1 packet) calamata olives, pitted

melted butter

Remove the hard ribs and chop spinach finely. Wash well in salted water and rinse in running cold water. Cook in a little boiling water until tender. Drain and cool. Sauté the onions and garlic in a little olive oil until translucent. Remove from the heat and allow to cool completely. Add to the spinach. Season with salt, pepper, nutmeg and origanum. Add the feta cheese and stir until well mixed. Spoon some filling onto the left-hand side of a sheet of phyllo pastry. Top with a few olives (about three per roll). Roll up the pastry while simultaneously folding in the sides to form a parcel. Deep-fry in hot oil until golden. Don't let the oil get too hot or bubbles will form in the pastry. Alternatively, you could brush each roll with melted butter and bake in a hot oven at 200 °C (400 °F) until golden brown and done.

Makes about 8-10 spinakopitas.

Bernard Estererer is the owner-chef of Bernard's Taphuis in Baron Van Rheede Street in Oudtshoorn. This Austrian chef knows all about cooking and has worked in many top-class restaurants in Europe. At his eatery he combines two cultures – South African food prepared with ingredients from the Little Karoo, but with a distinct Austrian flavour.

Quince strudel

Filling

1,5 kg quinces, wiped clean
    and cut into 3-mm slices
375 ml (1½ c) sugar
7 ml (1½ t) ground cinnamon
7 ml (1½ t) ground cloves
5 ml (1 t) vanilla essence
10 ml (2 t) Grand Marnier liqueur
60 ml (¼ c) butter
water

Crumble layer

200 ml sugar
500 ml (2 c) fresh breadcrumbs
100 ml butter

6 sheets phyllo pastry
melted butter

Preheat the oven to 180 °C (350 °F). Arrange the quinces for the filling in an oven dish, mix the rest of the filling ingredients and sprinkle over the top. Add a little water. Cover and bake in the oven until the quinces are done (this takes about 2 hours). Allow to cool.

Mix all the ingredients for the crumble layer together. Brush each phyllo sheet with melted butter and place 6 sheets on top of each other with crumble in between. Top with the filling and roll up. Brush the outside with the melted butter and bake until golden brown and done (about 20 minutes).

Serve slightly warmed, with cream.

Serves 6.

Fried ostrich liver with cognac

700 g ostrich liver, membrane and bigger veins removed

125 ml (½ c) olive oil

5 rashers bacon, cut into smaller pieces

250 ml (1 c) thinly sliced onion

250 ml (1 c) chicken stock

250 ml (1 c) cream

30 ml (2 T) crème fraîche or sour cream

50 ml cognac or 10-year-old brandy

balsamic vinegar

marjoram to taste

salt and freshly ground black pepper to taste

Cut the liver into 5-mm thick slices. Heat half the olive oil and fry the bacon lightly. Add the onion and stir-fry until translucent. Add the rest of the oil, heat and fry the liver until browned on the outside but still pink inside. Remove from the pan and set aside. Heat the chicken stock, cream, crème fraîche and cognac together and boil to reduce the sauce slightly. Add the liver mixture and heat through. Season with a good shot of balsamic vinegar, marjoram and salt and pepper to taste.

Serve with rice and vegetables.

Serves 4.

De Rust has a country store, Die Groen Bliktrommel. The name is a reminder of Ouma's worn but sturdy green tin trunk in which she stored food goodies up in the dark attic. Today travellers make a special detour to browse amongst the shelves packed with old-fashioned bric-a-brac and things to eat from the kitchens and vegetable gardens of the Little Karoo.

Ouma Bettie's ripe fig jam

Serve with home-made scones. The jam is made in the microwave oven.

1 kg peeled ripe figs

1 kg castor sugar

30 ml (2 T) lemon juice

piece crushed ginger

Place the figs in a 4-litre glass bowl, cover and microwave for 6 minutes on 100% power. Stir in the castor sugar, lemon juice and ginger. Mash the figs with a potato masher and microwave uncovered for 10 minutes on 50% power. Stir well. Microwave for another 30 minutes on 50% power, also uncovered, before spooning into clean, sterilised jars.

Makes about 1,5 kg jam.

Ouma Bettie's ripe fig jam, served with home-made scones

Aunt Maxie's tipsy tartlets

5 ml (1 t) bicarbonate of soda

250 g dates, cut into pieces

250 ml (1 c) boiling water

125 g margarine

250 ml (1 c) sugar

2 eggs, whisked

500 ml (2 c) cake flour

5 ml (1 t) baking powder

2 ml (½ t) salt

250 ml (1 c) chopped walnuts

SYRUP

300 ml sugar

15 ml (1 T) butter

180 ml (¾ c) water

pinch salt

5 ml (1 t) vanilla essence

125 ml (½ c) brandy

Preheat the oven to 180 °C (350 °F). Grease two muffin pans with butter or margarine or spray with nonstick spray.

Sprinkle the bicarbonate of soda over half the dates and pour the boiling water over. Stir and cool.

Beat the margarine and sugar together until creamy. Add the whisked eggs and mix well. Sift the dry ingredients together and fold into the sugar mixture. Add the remaining dates, the walnuts and the date mixture to the sugar mixture and mix. Spoon into the prepared muffin pans and bake for about 30 minutes, or until golden brown.

Boil all the ingredients for the syrup together and pour half the syrup over the tartlets when they come out of the oven. Pour the remaining syrup over the tartlets just before serving.

Makes 16 tartlets.

Calitzdorp is known as the port capital of the country, but here you will also find ostrich, orchard upon orchard of honey-sweet fruit, and an abundance of quinces. And you soon discover that the women of this region know how to transform these Little Karoo products into the most delectable dishes.

Just before entering Calitzdorp, you pass the turn-off to Welgevonden guesthouse. Briëtte Barry has converted the old homestead and outbuildings into a stylish establishment where she treats guests to local produce, served in all kinds of interesting ways.

Pan-fried beef fillet with port sauce

Briëtte likes to serve the fillet slices with port onions.

50 ml butter

50 ml oil

4-6 slices beef fillet, each
    about 2,5 cm thick

salt and black pepper (optional)

SAUCE

200 ml port

1 small onion

1 sprig fresh thyme

1 sprig fresh origanum

2 ml (½ t) meat stock powder

125 ml (½ c) cream

30 g butter

First make the sauce: Heat the port, onion and fresh herbs in a small saucepan, reducing the port by about three quarters. Remove the onion and herbs. Add the meat stock powder and cream. Bring to the boil again, stirring continuously. Add knobs of butter and mix well with a wire whisk after each addition.

Heat the butter and oil together in a pan and fry the fillets until nicely browned on the outside but still slightly pink inside, about 7 minutes altogether. Season with salt and black pepper, if preferred, and serve immediately with the port sauce.

Serves 4.

Port onions

500 g small onions, peeled

40 ml (8 t) olive oil

50 ml brown sugar

1 bay leaf

125 ml (½ c) port

Sauté the onions in the heated olive oil, along with the brown sugar and bay leaf, until pale brown. Add the port and simmer until the onions are soft.

Serve with the pan-fried fillet slices (p. 189), if preferred.

Serves 4-6.

Fig truffles

These delicious truffels made of dried figs are very quick to prepare. Serve them with coffee or a glass of port or sherry after the meal.

400-500 g dried figs

75 ml (5 T) port

50 ml desiccated coconut

100 g pecan nuts, coarsely
   chopped

150 ml condensed milk

400 g dark chocolate, broken
   into squares

Soak the figs overnight in the port. Chop finely in the food processor, add the coconut, pecan nuts and condensed milk and process until the mixture is well blended. Roll into small balls. Melt the chocolate in a glass bowl over a saucepan of boiling water or in the microwave oven, stirring occasionally. Dip the balls in the melted chocolate and leave until the chocolate has set.

Makes 60-70 balls.

Ria Oosthuizen of Gamka East, in the Calitzdorp district, is a first-rate cook and an expert on ostrich dishes and the foods of the district. She also likes to experiment with new ideas in her kitchen.

Onions and mushrooms in port

The dish keeps well in the fridge.

boiling water

500 g small onions

40 ml (8 t) butter or margarine

500 ml (2 c) port

250 g button mushrooms,
   wiped clean with a damp cloth

25 ml (5 t) tomato paste

2 medium tomatoes, skinned
   and coarsely chopped

salt and freshly ground black pepper
   to taste

15 ml (1 T) sugar

12,5 ml (2½ t) grape vinegar

Pour boiling water over the onions and leave for a while. Drain and remove the skins. Pat the onions dry.

Heat half the butter or margarine in a saucepan. Stir-fry the onions until they just begin to brown. Add the port and simmer slowly for 15-20 minutes. Stir-fry the mushrooms lightly in the remaining butter or margarine. Add the mushrooms and the remaining ingredients to the onions and simmer until soft but not mushy.

Serves 4-6.

Quince chutney with port

1,5 kg quinces, peeled, cored
    and cut into pieces
1 green sweet pepper, seeded and
    coarsely chopped
4 red chillies, seeded and chopped
500 g onions, cut into rings
300 ml water
6 cloves garlic, crushed
350 ml sultanas
about 800 ml brown sugar, to taste
15 ml (1 T) salt
15 ml (1 T) ground ginger
15 ml (1 T) ground coriander
5 ml (1 t) nutmeg
10 ml (2 t) black peppercorns
500 ml (2 c) port
200-250 ml grape vinegar
5-10 ml (1-2 t) cornflour if necessary

Place the quinces, sweet pepper, chillies, onions and water in a saucepan and simmer until the quinces are soft. Add the remaining ingredients and simmer until the chutney is no longer watery. Thicken with cornflour, mixed with a little water, if necessary. Taste and add more sugar or vinegar if needed.

Spoon into clean, sterilised jars and seal.

Makes about three 500-ml (2 c) jars.

Bottled quinces

1 kg quinces
500 ml (2 c) water
250 ml (1 c) sugar
2 pieces stick cinnamon
5 whole cloves

Peel and core the quinces and cut into pieces. To obtain a lovely red colour, peel them the night before and arrange on an uncovered tray.

Heat the water, sugar, cinnamon and cloves together. Stir to dissolve the sugar before the mixture comes to the boil and simmer well for about 1 minute. Add the quinces and boil until soft. Spoon into clean, sterilised jars and seal.

Makes three 500-ml (2 c) jars.

Leg of mutton in port and buttermilk

The gravy just makes this leg of mutton dish. If preferred, says Ria, make small incisions in the leg of mutton and insert a piece of bacon, a clove and a raisin in each.

1 leg of mutton, about 1,5 kg

MARINADE
250 ml (1 c) buttermilk
250 ml (1 c) oil
1 medium onion, finely chopped
10-15 ml (2-3 t) mustard powder
4 cloves garlic, crushed
salt and black pepper to taste

GRAVY
10-15 ml (2-3 t) cake flour
25 ml (5 t) finely chopped parsley
15 ml (1 T) prepared mustard
50 ml quince jelly
50 ml port
125 ml (½ c) cream

Place the leg of mutton in a stainless steel or glass dish. Mix all the ingredients for the marinade, except the salt and black pepper, and pour over the meat. Leave the meat in the marinade for 1-2 days, turning often.

Preheat the oven to 160 °C (325 °F). Remove the leg of mutton from the marinade, season with salt and black pepper and wrap in aluminium foil. Place the meat in a roasting pan and oven-roast for 40 minutes for each 500 g plus 40 minutes extra. Unwrap the foil during the last 30 minutes of the cooking time to allow the leg to brown. Place the meat on a serving platter and keep warm in the warming drawer.

Reduce the pan juices and thicken with cake flour mixed with a little water. Add the remaining gravy ingredients and heat until the gravy comes to the boil and thickens. Serve the dish with bottled quinces (p. 191).

Serves about 8.

The warm-hearted Karoo

The Karoo has a way of silently communicating with you – and capturing your heart in the process. You smell the earth and the plants and feast your eyes on wide expanses studded with rocky hills and bare poplar trees silhouetted against a blue sky, with perhaps a fleecy cloud here and there. This is wide-open country; here you can breathe freely.

A visit to the Karoo is both special and unforget-table. Whether you overnight at Colesberg or Graaff-Reinet, seeing the moonlight shining on the tranquil waters of the Orange River on a perfect winter's night, or looking out over the Valley of Desolation, you can't help but realise that the Karoo is a place of endless enchantment. Here you can watch dassies and klipspringers on the hillsides, or relax around a fire to discuss the day's hunt and, in the course of the conversation, find out where the fish eagle has its nest.

In years gone by, large herds of game roamed the Karoo plains. Blue wildebeest and hartebeest were a common sight, but now only smaller game like grey rheebok and springbok are left. Fortunately, farmers are beginning to introduce game on a large scale and the Karoo is once again home to many antelope species – from kudu to eland and gemsbok. In recent years it has also become a popular destination for game hunters from overseas.

But this is also sheep country, with meat the likes of which few of us have ever tasted. Karoo mutton is known for its flavour and tenderness. I've been told, however, that not all Karoo mutton tastes the same; in the Colesberg district many herbs – such as thyme, rosemary and the mints – grow in the veld, and the meat absorbs the flavours of the bushes the sheep feed on. Renosterbos (rhinoceros bush) ensures the animals remain in good condition.

Karoo towns like Graaff-Reinet and Colesberg induce feelings of nostalgia for the past. As the fourth-oldest town in the country, Graaff-Reinet has a rich cultural heritage and boasts more than two hundred houses which have been declared national monuments. No wonder that it is known as the jewel of the Karoo. Colesberg lies in the heart of the Karoo, halfway between Cape Town and the north. Its hotchpotch of typical Karoo flat-roofed houses and Cape Dutch, Victorian and Georgian styles tells a tale of great battles between the Boers and the English during the Anglo-Boer War.

In and around these Karoo towns there are now countless stopovers, eating and holiday establishments where you can enjoy the genuine hospitality and the tranquillity, and where the ancient church clock reminds you of the time every half-hour – although in these peaceful surroundings you are disinclined to take much notice of it.

There is no shortage of restaurants in Colesberg. Bordeaux and Ketelfontein provide breakfast or tea and cake; the Tuiskoop and Karoonessie offer delicious home-baked goods, and at the Horse & Mill Pub you can enjoy a light lunch or home-made soup. At night, the Plattelander and Upstairs Restaurants welcome you with Karoo food and "local-is-lekker" on the menu. Outside the town you can spend the night in a tent house on the banks of the Orange River or at any of the numerous guest farms.

Coniston House, one of the fine historic homes in Colesberg, has been converted into a guesthouse. Built by Thomas Plewman in 1835, this ochre-coloured double-storeyed house with its Tuscan-blue shutters is one of the very few authentic Cape Georgian homes in Colesberg. During the Boer War it was used as a hospital, and negotiations between President Kruger and the British took place here.

The house still belongs to some of Plewman's descendants, the Southey family. Tony, Michael and Liz Southey transformed it into a stylish bed and breakfast establishment.

Griddlecakes

700 g (5 c) cake flour

salt to taste

5 g (½ packet) instant yeast

lukewarm water

Mix the cake flour, salt and yeast together and add just enough water to form a soft dough. Knead the dough for about 15 minutes until smooth and elastic, place in a greased bowl and leave in a warm place to rise until doubled in volume. Punch down gently and shape into small balls. Leave to rise once more before placing on the grid over medium-hot coals. Braai until done, turning the cakes occasionally.

Serve with mineola preserve (p. 198).

Makes 20 small griddlecakes.

Mineola preserve

Liz Southey serves this preserve for breakfast.

1 kg (5-6) whole mineolas

1 kg white sugar

1,5 litres (6 c) water

juice of half a lemon

Gently scrape the rind of the mineolas with a fork or piece of glass. Cut a cross in the bottom of each mineola and place the fruit in a large bowl. Cover with water and soak for 1 day.

Pour off the water, cover the fruit with fresh water and soak for another day. Pour off the water once more and gently squeeze the fruit to remove excess water and pips. Cut the fruit in half horizontally and cut into rough wedges. Place the fruit in a stainless steel saucepan.

Heat the sugar and water, stirring until the sugar has dissolved, and bring to the boil. Simmer for about 5 minutes and pour over the fruit. Cool the fruit in the syrup overnight.

The next day, bring the syrup and fruit to the boil and simmer slowly for 20 minutes. Cover and leave the fruit in the syrup for two days.

On the last day, add the lemon juice and slowly simmer the fruit until the syrup is golden and thickens slightly and the fruit is translucent. Transfer to sterilised jars while still hot and seal immediately.

Makes about 1 litre (4 c) of preserve.

Leg of venison with lavender

Grassridge has been the Southey family farm for generations. Liz Southey does not visit their Karoo farm regularly, but over the years she has perfected her venison-cooking skills. In any event, she has always been an excellent cook who likes to experiment with different flavours. She has written many food articles for various magazines and newspapers and has also done the styling of food photographs for *You*, among others.

Liz reveals this dish came about quite by accident. She'd asked her husband, Michael, to pick a few sprigs of rosemary but, because it was dark, he returned with lavender.

1 leg of venison, about 1,5-2 kg

2 cloves garlic, thinly sliced

2 sprigs fresh lavender and extra
  for gravy and garnishing

250 g (1 packet) back bacon

2 medium onions, skinned and halved

olive oil

salt and coarsely ground black pepper

boiling water

red wine

5 ml (1 t) quince or kumquat jelly

cornflour to thicken gravy

Preheat the oven to 160 °C (325 °F).

Make rows of incisions all over the leg, each about 6 cm deep. Insert slivers of garlic into the first row and pieces of lavender into the second. Repeat until all the incisions are filled. Cover the leg with rashers of bacon, overlapping slightly, and secure with cocktail sticks. Place the leg in a deep oven pan and surround with the onions. Sprinkle with olive oil and season with salt and pepper. Oven-roast for 1½ hours until tender and done. (Remove the bacon 30 minutes before the end of the cooking time and chop finely.) Reset the oven to 200 °C (400 °F) and brown the leg. Remove from the oven and place in the warming drawer for about 20 minutes.

To the pan juices add a little boiling water, red wine to taste, quince jelly and a few sprigs of lavender. Cook until thickened and the flavours have developed. Thicken with cornflour, mixed with a little water.

Serve the leg with the gravy and oven-roasted vegetables. Serves 8.

Leg of venison with lavender

Taetse and Legonda Voster started Ketelfontein Nursery as a hobby. At first it was on their farm, Ketelfontein, where they keep merinos and cattle. Later they moved the nursery into town and also opened a tea garden where their guests can indulge in milk tart, orange and chocolate cakes, a variety of filled pancakes and toasted sandwiches.

Milk tart

CRUST

250 ml (1 c) cake flour

15 ml (3 t) baking powder

pinch salt

90 ml (6 T) butter, diced

1 egg yolk

about 30 ml (2 T) water

FILLING

30 ml (2 T) butter

45 ml (3 T) cake flour

pinch salt

375 ml (1½ c) hot milk

45-60 ml (3-4 T) sugar (or to taste)

2 extra-large eggs, separated

3 ml (generous ½ t) almond, orange or vanilla essence

sugar and ground cinnamon for sprinkling on top

Preheat the oven to 190 °C (375 °F) and grease a medium-sized pie dish with butter or margarine or spray with nonstick spray.

First prepare the crust: Sift the dry ingredients together and rub in the butter with your fingertips until the mixture resembles coarse breadcrumbs. Cut the egg yolk and water into the flour mixture and mix to form a soft pastry. Wrap in plastic wrap and chill for 30 minutes. Take out of the fridge to soften slightly before rolling out. Roll out the pastry and line the pie dish with it. Prick the bottom gently and chill.

Make the filling: Melt the butter in a medium-sized saucepan and sprinkle the flour and salt on top. Simmer slowly for a minute, stirring continuously. Remove from the stove.

Beat the hot milk and sugar together and gradually beat into the flour mixture. Heat slowly, stirring continuously, until the mixture comes to the boil and thickens. Beat a little of the milk mixture into the egg yolks, add the essence and then beat into the remaining milk mixture.

Beat the egg whites until stiff and fold into the mixture. Pour into the prepared crust and bake for 25-30 minutes until cooked and firm. Sprinkle with a little sugar and ground cinnamon and serve lukewarm.

Makes 1 milk tart.

At the Horse & Mill Pub, Dave and Thelma Weideman welcome you to what must be the only pub in the country boasting an old horse-driven mill wheel. The building started life as a coach house in the 1840's and the horse-driven mill wheel originally came from the farm Sewefontein. In the convivial atmosphere of this historic building, guests feast on delicious vegetable soup with home-baked bread and on peri-peri chicken livers.

Vegetable soup

A wonderfully wholesome veggie soup. Add water if you prefer a thinner soup. Theresa serves it at the Pub with her scrumptious home-baked brown bread.

6 medium carrots, scraped and diced

1 medium onion, finely chopped

1 small cauliflower, broken into florets

4 stalks celery, finely chopped

4 medium potatoes, grated

500 ml (2 c) dried peas, soaked in water
  for 30 minutes

2 tomato paste cubes

1 medium butternut, peeled and diced

45 ml (3 T) vegetable stock powder

250 ml (1 c) small pasta shapes (optional)

2 handfuls chopped fresh parsley

grated rind of 1 lemon

salt and freshly ground black pepper to taste

Place all the ingredients, except the parsley and seasonings, in a large saucepan. Add about 7 x 250 ml (7 c) water or enough to cover the vegetables and bring to the boil. Reduce the temperature and simmer slowly until the peas are soft and done. Add more water if preferred.

Add the parsley and lemon rind, season generously with salt and black pepper and serve hot.

Serves 16.

The most delicious home-baked goods produced by Colesberg's expert bakers are sold at the Tuiskoop. This home industry was started during the years of drought and was one of the first in the country. Salomé du Plessis and Aunt Bella Havenga, who is well over eighty years old, were two of the founder members.

Tuiskoop's savoury bites

A Salomé du Plessis speciality.

250 g Cheddar cheese, grated
250 g cake flour
250 g (½ brick) butter
pinch cayenne pepper
2 ml (½ t) salt
Marmite

Place all the ingredients, except the Marmite, in a food processor and process to form a soft dough. Gather the dough into a ball, wrap in plastic wrap and chill until firm.

Meanwhile, preheat the oven to 150 °C (300 °F). Roll small pieces of dough into small balls (about 1-1,25 cm in diameter) and arrange on baking sheets. Chill once more. Bake until done and a pale straw colour, about 7 minutes. Cool completely before sandwiching together with Marmite.

Serve as snacks with drinks.

Makes about 100 bites.

It took months of backbreaking work to restore the Victorian house in Church Street to its former glory, says Elsabé Engelbrecht, owner of Bordeaux.

The house dates back to 1835, and was occupied for many years. A large number of the previous owners' descendants still live in the town. Within the first week after opening, they had to convert the place into a restaurant with seating for forty guests, due to the great demand for traditional boerekos.

Elsabé also likes trying cake and tart recipes and adapting them to her taste.

Lucerne stew

Elsabé Engelbrecht was born in the Free State and has always loved to cook. She points out that not only sheep eat lucerne – it can also be used in stews. Use spinach if lucerne is unobtainable, she says.

olive oil
60 ml (¼ c) cake flour
few sprigs fresh thyme
salt and coarsely ground
　black pepper
500 g stewing mutton, cubed
2 large onions, coarsely chopped
2 cloves garlic, crushed
125 ml (½ c) hot water
4 medium potatoes, peeled
　and cubed
4 x 250 ml (4 c) chopped lucerne
　greens or spinach
grated rind of 1 lemon
25 ml (5 t) tomato sauce
few drops Worcester sauce

Heat the olive oil in a medium-sized saucepan. Mix the cake flour, fresh thyme leaves, salt and black pepper and roll the cubed meat in the mixture. Brown the meat in the heated olive oil and drain on paper towelling. Heat a small amount of oil and sauté the onions and garlic in the same saucepan until tender and fragrant. Add the meat cubes, water and potato cubes, reduce the heat and simmer slowly for about 1 hour until the meat is tender. Add the lucerne to the meat mixture. Simmer until done and add the lemon rind, tomato sauce and Worcester sauce to taste. Season to taste with more salt and generous amounts of coarsely ground black pepper. Serve with rice or samp.

Serves 4-6.

Lucerne stew

Sosatie game sausage

10 kg venison, e.g. springbok

2,5 kg bacon or sheep's tails

125-130 ml (about ½ c) salt

25 ml (5 t) pepper

75-100 ml curry powder

25 ml (5 t) Fondor

30 ml (2 T) chutney

75-125 ml (5 T-½ c) brown vinegar

750 ml (3 c) red wine

10 kg mutton fat or pork lard, finely diced

500-700 g cleaned casings

Cube the meat and bacon and add the rest of the ingredients, except the fat and casings. Mix well and leave to marinate for 1-2 hours. Add the fat and mince everything together. (Do not handle the meat too much.) Place the casings over the sausage attachment of the mincer and stuff with meat mixture. Roll up, place in plastic bags and freeze until needed.

Cook over medium coals and serve with griddlecakes and green fig preserve.

Makes about 20 kg raw sausage.

The Upstairs restaurant is located above Nommerpasskoene, and both belong to Marianne du Plessis. This Capetonian likes to entertain, and soon after the first guesthouses opened in Colesberg she realised it was the right time to open a restaurant. The delicacies on the menu include mussel soup and lamb pie, and even "local-is-lekker", a freshly prepared waffle served with ice cream and caramel sauce. Upstairs Restaurant in Colesberg becomes a popular gathering place when bikers pass through town on their way to the annual Buffalo Rally, or when the time draws near for the Argus Cycling Tour and Two Oceans Marathon in Cape Town.

Lamb pie

At the Upstairs restaurant the puff pastry shells for the pies are baked separately and placed on top of each pie before serving.

1 kg boned lamb cubes

oil

5 ml (1 t) ground coriander

3 ml (generous ½ t) mustard powder

15 ml (1 T) vinegar

7 peppercorns

1 small onion studded with 5 cloves

about 500 ml (2 c) water

500 g frozen vegetables

7 ml (1½ t) mushroom soup powder

7 ml (1½ t) cornflour

7 ml (1½ t) gravy thickener (Bisto)

250 ml (1 c) water

pinch sugar

a generous dash of lemon juice and a little
  grated rind

salt and freshly ground black pepper to taste

1 roll (400 g) frozen puff pastry, thawed

egg yolk and water mixture

Lightly brown the meat in a little oil. Add the seasonings, onion and 500 ml (2 c) water and simmer slowly for about 30 minutes, or until the meat is tender. Add the vegetables and simmer for about 20 minutes, or until the vegetables are heated through and done, but still slightly crisp. Blend the soup powder, cornflour and gravy thickener with 250 ml (½ c) water and add. Season with sugar, lemon juice and rind, and salt and pepper to taste. Bring to the boil and simmer for about 5 minutes. Transfer the filling to a large ovenproof dish or small dishes and cool completely.

Preheat the oven to 200 °C (400 °F). Roll out the pastry and place over the pie filling. Press the sides down, pierce the crust in one or two places to allow the steam to escape and brush with egg yolk and water mixture. Bake until the crust is nicely puffed up and golden brown and the pie is hot.

Makes a large pie.

Lamb pie

Andries and Orpie van Niekerk of Rooidam make the most delicious sosaties using Dorper meat – at a small-stock show in Bloemfontein they made 6 000 sosaties and people asked for more. And their sosaties are much in demand whenever there is a fête in Colesberg.

Leg of mutton sosaties

MARINADE

50 ml peach or apricot jam

75 ml (5 T) mild curry powder

75 ml (5 T) sugar

125 ml (½ c) cake flour

2 ml (½ t) turmeric

5 ml (1 t) Worcester sauce

2 ml (½ t) ground ginger

2 ml (½ t) ground cinnamon

125 ml (½ c) milk

125 ml (½ c) grape vinegar

1 tin (385 g) pie apples

1 green sweet pepper, seeded and
   cut into pieces

4 onions, coarsely chopped

1 kg leg of mutton, cubed

salt and coarsely ground black pepper

Using a nonmetallic dish, blend all the marinade ingredients together and mix with the pie apples, sweet pepper, onions and meat cubes. Marinate for about two days and thread the meat onto skewers. Season with salt and pepper and braai over the coals until done.

Makes about 6 portions.

In the Colesberg district there are world-class horse studs – such as the one on Terry and Barbara Silcock's farm Starston, where three generations of Terry's family have bred horses.

This is also a guest farm, where hunters come in winter to practise their sport. They are treated to the most delectable venison dishes, of course, and even today guests still feast on leg of venison, prepared the way Terry's late mother, Barbara, made it. Naturally, her famous preserves or quince jellies were served with this dish; she even pickled walnuts.

Karoo leg of venison with creamy raisin sauce

1 leg of venison
bacon, cut into small pieces
slivers of fresh garlic

MARINADE
500-750 ml (2-3 c) red wine
125 ml (½ c) brown vinegar
6-8 whole allspice berries
4 bay leaves
about 6 whole cloves
a few pieces cassia or cinnamon sticks
about 10 black peppercorns

GLAZE
45-60 ml (3-4 T) apricot jam
30 ml (2 T) Worcester sauce
coarsely ground black pepper
2 ml (½ t) nutmeg
5 ml (1 t) ground cinnamon
5 ml (1 t) allspice

250 g bacon rashers

GRAVY
about 250 ml (1 c) marinade
250 ml (1 c) cream
125 ml (½ c) raisins or sultanas
gravy powder or cornflour

Make small incisions in the leg of venison and insert a piece of bacon and a garlic sliver into each. Place the leg in a large nonmetallic dish and add all the marinade ingredients. Leave for two days, turning every day. (Do not place the leg in the fridge in cold weather.) After two days, remove the leg from the dish and place it in a large roasting pan. Reserve the marinade.

Mix the glaze ingredients and coat each rasher of bacon with this mixture. Arrange the rashers over the leg, making sure they overlap. Secure both ends of each rasher with cocktail sticks. Brush with the rest of the glaze mixture.

Mix the marinade, cream and raisins or sultanas and add to the roasting pan. Cover the pan with aluminium foil and oven-roast at 160 °C (325 °F) for about 2 hours. Remove the foil and baste the leg occasionally, taking care not to remove the glaze. If the gravy mixture is too dry, add the rest of the marinade. Insert a skewer into the thickest part of the meat to test for doneness; if the meat juices run pink, return to the oven.

When tender and cooked through, remove the foil and brown the leg under the grill. Remove the leg from the pan. Thicken the pan juices with a little gravy powder or cornflour, mixed with a little water, and serve with the meat.

Serves 8.

Variation: Add a packet of mixed dried fruit to the pan during the baking process. They add a wonderful flavour and improve the appearance of the dish.

Leg of lamb with port stuffing

Barbara serves only yellow rice and vegetables with this stuffed leg. Anything more will spoil that exceptional Karoo flavour, she says.

STUFFING
knob of butter
750 ml (3 c) brown breadcrumbs
½ medium onion, chopped
2 cloves garlic, crushed
15 ml (1 T) chopped fresh parsley
5 ml (1 t) fresh or dried rosemary
5 ml (1 t) fresh or dried thyme
1 ml (¼ t) grated lemon rind
30 ml (2 T) lemon juice
30 ml (2 T) chutney
salt and coarsely ground black pepper to taste
125 ml (½ c) chopped walnuts
125 ml (½ c) port or sherry
1-2 extra-large eggs

1 leg of lamb
500 ml (2 c) vegetable or meat stock
15 ml (1 T) chopped mint

Preheat the oven to 160 °C (325 °F).

Melt the butter in a pan and lightly fry the breadcrumbs. Add the onion and garlic and fry slowly until tender. (Add more butter if necessary.) Remove from the stove and add the remaining stuffing ingredients. Add one egg and mix, adding the extra egg to bind the mixture if necessary.

Neatly bone and butterfly the leg of lamb, skin side facing down. Spread the stuffing over the meat, leaving a border of about 2 cm uncovered to allow for the filling to expand during cooking.

Roll up the meat and secure it with string at about 2-cm intervals. Place the meat in an oven pan. Pour over the stock and sprinkle with the mint. Oven-roast for about 1 hour and 45 minutes (20 minutes for every 500 g of meat plus 20 minutes extra).

Brown under the oven grill and leave to cool slightly before slicing thinly – an electric carving knife works best. Garnish the carved meat with a few sprigs of mint. Add a little boiling water to the pan juices and bring to the boil to form a flavoursome gravy. Serve with meat and vegetables.

Everyone in Colesberg simply calls it Neels's butchery. Of course, this is Neels Snyman's place, which was once a dance hall and now sells every conceivable speciality – from venison to sosaties, polonies, boerewors, biltong and dried sausage, each made according to Neels's own recipe. He buys from the district only and does his own slaughtering.

Springbok with marrow bones

Neels's wife, Bets, says she likes venison prepared this way – and it's even more delicious with the marrow bones added.

2 springbok necks, sawed into pieces
600 g marrow bones, sawed into pieces
1 medium onion, chopped
1 beef stock cube
500 ml (2 c) water
2 ml (½ t) nutmeg
2 ml (½ t) ground cloves
5 ml (1 t) coarsely ground black pepper
10 ml (2 t) salt
50 ml vinegar
50 ml port

Place all the ingredients in a large saucepan and bring to the boil. Reduce the heat, cover and simmer until the meat is tender and falls off the bones. Remove most of the small bones, reserving the marrow bones. Adjust seasoning to taste, and serve with quince jelly and boiled potatoes seasoned with a sprinkling of nutmeg.

Serves 4-6.

Springbok with marrow bones

Belinda Gordon, from the Colesberg information office, lived in Natal for a long time. About ten years ago she and her husband went to Colesberg and moved into an old house which they restored beautifully. She says they've never once longed for the green fields of Natal. Belinda is enthusiastic about Colesberg, especially about its role in the Anglo-Boer War. She's writing a book on the subject and she also has an Internet website about Colesberg.

Peruvian tripe

Belinda's husband, Harry, is Peruvian by descent, and she likes to use the flavours of that country's cuisine in her cooking. Here, tripe is flavoured with cumin and served with paper-thin potato crisps and handfuls of parsley. A really unusual dish!

750 g sheep's tripe, scrubbed
  and rinsed in cold water
5 ml (1 t) salt
15 ml (1 T) lemon juice
olive oil
1 large onion, sliced into thin rings
2-3 cloves garlic, crushed
chilli to taste, seeded and chopped
5 ml (1 t) ground cumin (jeera)
5 ml (1 t) grape vinegar
salt and freshly ground black pepper
6 medium potatoes, peeled and
  cut into paper-thin strips
good quantity fresh parsley, chopped
125 ml (½ c) grated Cheddar cheese

Cover the tripe with cold water, and add the salt and lemon juice. Cover and simmer for about 2-3 hours until tender. Drain and cut into very thin strips.

Heat olive oil and fry the tripe, onion, garlic and chilli until the onion is fragrant and soft. Add the cumin and grape vinegar and heat for about 1 minute. Season generously with salt and pepper and keep warm.

Fry the potato strips in olive oil until lightly browned and drain on paper towelling. Add the potato strips, parsley and cheese just before serving.

Serves 4.

Ivan and Marleze Sinclair have always loved the bush and camping. When Ivan settled on the farm, he set up his own tent camp on the banks of the Orange River. De Oude Pomp's luxurious safari tents are snugly tucked away among the bushes on the river banks. The old pump station next to it has been beautifully renovated and fitted out for additional accommodation. Ivan did all the construction work; Marleze provides the Karoo cuisine.

Venison stroganoff

1 medium onion, finely chopped
1 clove garlic, crushed
oil
1 tin (285 g) mushrooms
1-1,5 kg venison, cooked until very tender and flaked
1 beef stock cube, dissolved in 250 ml (1 c) water
15 ml (1 T) sherry
250 ml (1 c) sour cream
5 ml (1 t) Worcester sauce
5 ml (1 t) Aromat
1 small tin (65 g) tomato paste
salt and pepper to taste
cornflour (optional)

Sauté the onion and garlic in a little oil until softened. Add the mushrooms and fry gently. Add the meat. Mix the rest of the ingredients, except the salt and pepper, add to the meat mixture and bring to the boil. Reduce the heat and simmer until the sauce is thickened and tasty. Season to taste with salt and pepper and thicken with a little cornflour, mixed with a little water, if necessary.

Serve with rice and a salad.

Serves 6.

On Arundel's back stoep you will find lots of farm cats basking in the sun all day long, hoping for scraps from the kitchen. Manie and Cornelia Wium farm sheep, but in winter, during the hunting season, Cornelia has to cater for large groups of hunters who stay at the farm. Her father-in-law started preparing chine – cured for biltong – like steaks, she says, and now it has become their speciality.

Pan-fried chine biltong

Cornelia always keeps a few pieces of cured chine, meant for biltong, to pan-fry like steaks, so a recipe for biltong is also included here.

BILTONG

40 kg chine of venison, sliced
   into strips for biltong

BILTONG MIXTURE

1 kg coarse salt
roasted coriander to taste
125 ml (½ c) brown sugar
50 ml black pepper
500 ml (2 c) brown vinegar

PAN-FRIED BILTONG

butter or margarine for frying
red wine
fresh thyme

Layer the biltong strips in a nonmetallic container. Sprinkle the ingredients for the biltong mixture over each layer. Leave for 48 hours, turning after 24 hours. Hang up to dry, reserving a few strips for frying. (The strips may also be frozen.)

Slice the biltong into pieces about 1,5-2 cm thick (allow 2 per person) and sauté on both sides in a little butter or margarine until browned. Do not overcook. Remove from the pan and set aside. Add a little red wine to the pan juices and simmer until the sauce is reduced. Season to taste with fresh thyme.

Anton du Plessis of Twyfelspoort owns Lady Laatvy, a double-deck launch on which you can explore the Orange River. Lining the river are towering cliffs, some of which resemble rocks stacked on top of one another. On closer inspection, one of them looks exactly like a Voortrekker woman wearing a bonnet. While the launch glides through the tranquil waters, Anton starts the braai and his wife, Juanita, is in the tiny galley preparing the starter – pan-fried barbel.

Braaied leg of venison

Anton du Plessis enjoys this method of preparing a leg of venison, which he learnt from neighbours Hennie and Antoinette Havenga.

MARINADE
250 ml (1 c) olive oil
250 ml (1 c) lemon juice
30 ml (2 T) Aromat
5 ml (1 t) chopped fresh rosemary
freshly ground black pepper

1 boned leg of venison (springbok
  or rheebok), stuffed with pork lard or bacon
salt

Mix the ingredients for the marinade. Place the leg in a nonmetallic container and add the marinade. Chill for 12 to 24 hours, turning occasionally. Remove and braai over medium-hot coals, seasoning with salt just before cooked through.
   Serve with griddlecakes, apricot jam and a salad.
   Serves 6-8.

Graaff-Reinet has been harbouring a gourmet treasure for quite some time now: the Andries Stockenström dining room and guesthouse. For three consecutive years it was named the best guesthouse, offering full service, in the country. André and Beatrice Barnard converted an old mansion, which dates back to the early nineteenth century, into a guesthouse where visitors can dine every night in true French style. Beatrice is a gourmet chef who received her training at the Ritz Hotel in France. She prepares dinner herself every night, using Karoo produce such as venison, lamb, prickly pears or quinces, as well as ingredients from her garden. Everything grows here, she says, from herbs to a wide variety of salad ingredients. There are also several fruit trees, such as fig, orange, plum, guava and even almond trees. All this bounty finds its way into her cooking, and she has a knack for creating unique dishes that are a feast for eye and palate. Each meal is a taste sensation, with flavours, textures and colours complementing one another perfectly.

Baked avocado with prawns and white-wine dressing

This starter was created in an emergency, says Beatrice. The combination of flavours is unsurpassable.

DRESSING

250 ml (1 c) white wine

125 ml (½ c) apple juice

60 ml (¼ c) dry Cinzano

1 bay leaf

250 ml (1 c) cream

2 ripe avocados, skinned, stoned
  and halved

4 slices white bread

olive oil

dried mixed herbs

mayonnaise

1 packet (230 g) frozen prawns

oil

mustard greens or mixed salad leaves

Preheat the oven to 180 °C (350 °F). Grease a baking sheet with butter or margarine or spray with nonstick spray.

Place all the dressing ingredients except the cream in a fairly small saucepan and bring to the boil. Boil until most of the liquid has evaporated and the mixture has been reduced to about 50 ml. Reduce the heat and add the cream. Simmer slowly until the sauce begins to change colour. Set aside.

Place an avocado half, cut side down, on top of each slice of bread and trim the bread following the outline of the avocado. Remove the avocado halves and brush the bread shapes lightly with olive oil and sprinkle with the dried mixed herbs. Return the avocado halves to the bread shapes and brush well with mayonnaise. Bake the avocados for 15 minutes or until the mayonnaise just begins to change colour. Remove immediately.

Meanwhile, stir-fry the prawns in a little oil until done. Arrange the lettuce leaves on four plates and place the avocado halves on top. Pour over the dressing and surround with the prawns. Serve immediately.

Serves 4.

Rolled lamb with spinach stuffing

1 saddle or loin of lamb, about 2 kg,
  boned

salt

mustard powder

STUFFING

oil

2 medium onions, finely chopped

4 cloves garlic, crushed

1 bunch (300 g) spinach, shredded

500 ml (2 c) fresh breadcrumbs

1 extra-large egg, whisked

10 ml (2 t) freshly chopped rosemary

salt and freshly ground black pepper

Preheat the oven to 160 °C (325 °F). Open out the joint and season the inside with salt and mustard powder.

Heat a little oil and sauté the onions and garlic until soft and translucent. Add the spinach, heating it until it wilts. Remove from the heat and add the breadcrumbs, egg and rosemary. Season with salt and black pepper and mix.

Spoon the stuffing on top of the meat and roll up. Secure with pieces of string and place on the rack of an oven-roasting pan. Oven-roast for 1½-2 hours or until done. Rest the meat for about 15 minutes before carving.

Serve with roast potatoes and sautéed baby vegetables.
Serves 6-8.

Pear salad with blue-cheese dressing

A mouthwatering combination of flavours.

DRESSING
250 ml (1 c) cream
30 ml (2 T) blue cheese
10 ml (2 t) dried tarragon (optional)

2 pears, peeled, halved and cored
pinch salt
1 packet mixed salad leaves with herbs
few walnut halves

Place the cream and blue cheese in a saucepan and heat slowly until reduced by half. Season with tarragon if preferred.

Place the pears in a saucepan and add just enough water to cover them halfway. Add a pinch of salt and boil until just tender but still firm. Drain and cool.

Arrange the salad leaves on four plates and place the pears on top. Pour over the dressing and surround with a few walnut halves.

Serves 4.

Kudu slices on rösti

Ensure the game has been well ripened. If you don't have ring forms for frying the potato rounds, shape the grated potatoes into rounds with a spoon and fry. Otherwise, use flat tins like tuna tins, cut open on both sides.

GARLIC SAUCE
125 ml (½ c) chopped garlic
250 ml (1 c) cream

6 medium potatoes, peeled and
    coarsely grated
oil
salt
1 loin of kudu, sliced into six 5-cm
    thick slices
rashers of bacon

Slowly heat the garlic and cream, simmering until the garlic is tender. Add salt to taste. Set aside and keep warm.

Squeeze the potato to remove any excess moisture. Place 6 small metal ring forms in a pan and add enough oil to cover the ring forms three quarters of the way. Heat the oil until hot and spoon the potato into the forms, spreading evenly with a spatula or spoon. Fry until the potato cakes just turn brown, turn and fry until done. Remove from the pan and drain on paper towelling.

Lightly oil a ribbed cast-iron pan and heat until very hot. Wrap each kudu slice in a rasher of bacon and fry in the heated pan until rare or medium-done. (It takes about 5 minutes on each side for medium-done.)

Place a potato cake on each heated dinner plate and place a kudu slice on top. Pour the garlic sauce around it and serve with vegetables in season.

Serves 6.

Rice pudding

Serve the rice pudding with quinces or oranges cooked in a syrup. Bake the rice pudding in individual moulds or a large dish.

500 ml (2 c) milk
250 ml (1 c) cream
100 ml sugar
4 extra-large eggs
2 egg yolks
pinch salt
5 ml (1 t) vanilla essence
grated rind of 1 orange
500 ml (2 c) cooked rice

Preheat the oven to 160 °C (325 °F). Grease a 30 cm x 20 cm oven dish with butter or margarine or spray with nonstick spray.

Beat together all the ingredients except the rice. Stir in the rice and turn the mixture into the oven dish. Place the dish in an oven pan filled halfway with hot water and bake for 40 minutes or until cooked and set. Serve hot with oranges or quinces in spicy syrup.

Serves 6-8.

Oranges or quinces in spicy syrup

Beatrice also cooks other whole fruit such as pears or guavas in the syrup and then serves the fruit with yoghurt for breakfast.

375 ml (1½ c) sugar
500 ml (2 c) water
3-4 pieces star anise
1 clove
1 cinnamon stick
2 oranges or quinces,
   peeled and sliced

Mix the sugar and water in a saucepan and add the star anise, clove and cinnamon. Heat, stirring until the sugar has dissolved, and bring to the boil. Add the oranges or quinces and simmer until the fruit is tender and glossy but still whole.
Serve as suggested.
Serves 4-6.

Tarte Tatin

Beatrice got the recipe for this typically French upside-down apple tart in Paris.

PASTRY
500 ml (2 c) cake flour
125 g butter, softened
1 egg yolk
45 ml (3 T) castor sugar
3 ml (generous ½ t) salt
45-60 ml (3-4 T) cold water

150 g butter
500 ml (2 c) sugar
2,5 kg Golden Delicious apples,
   peeled, cored and halved

Preheat the oven to 180 °C (350 °F). Sift the flour in a mixing bowl and make a hollow in the centre. Add the butter, egg yolk, castor sugar, salt and 45 ml (3 T) cold water. Mix well and then work in the flour until the mixture forms coarse crumbs. Add more water if necessary. Gather the pastry into a ball and press with the heel of your hand until it is soft and pliable. The pastry should not be moist or sticky. Chill until needed.
Slice the 150 g butter into thin slices and spread evenly in the bottom of a 23-cm round cake tin with thick sides. Sprinkle with 500 ml (2 c) sugar. Arrange the apples on top in concentric circles, covering the surface of the tin. Heat on top of the stove for about 10-15 minutes or until a light caramel syrup is formed. Place the cake tin with the apples in the bottom half of the oven and bake for 20 minutes. Cool slightly so the steam can escape.
Roll the pastry into a circle large enough to cover the cake tin and chill for 15 minutes. Cover the apples with the pastry circle, folding the edge in, and bake for about 30 minutes, or until the crust is golden brown and done. Remove from the oven and cool until lukewarm.
Carefully turn out the tart so the crust is at the bottom. Remove any apples that remain stuck to the bottom of the tin with a spatula and arrange on the crust.
The tart may be prepared 6-8 hours in advance and kept at room temperature. Serve hot with cream in a separate container.
Makes a large tart.

Tarte Tatin

Bush
cuisine

The Phalaborwa region in the Northern Province is one of dramatic contrasts. Bound by Magoebas Kloof in the west and the Blyde River Canyon in the south, the majestic Drakensberg keeps a constant vigil further south. Then, suddenly, you find yourself in the Lowveld wilderness with its world-renowned Kruger National Park stretching northwards.

When you drive along the R40 towards Hoedspruit, you realise that this is game country. The road virtually cuts the game reserves in two, with high fences on either side, although these are said to be less than effective in confining game. It is early morning, but already you experience the feeling of freedom that only the wilderness can provide – small warthogs, tails erect, dart across the road in single file and waterbuck and giraffe look up, piqued, at your approach. The quiet is almost palpable . . . here, the things that really matter are determined by the course of nature.

Phalaborwa is rightly known as the gateway to game and golf; not only is the well-known Phalaborwa Gate to the Kruger National Park just outside the town, but it also boasts a unique golf course at the Hans Merensky Country Club, where golfers regularly encounter wild animals, and crocodiles and hippopotami hide in water holes. A leopard or lion kill on the fairway is quite common, and elephants have taken up residence in the grounds of the large copper mine outside the town.

The Phalaborwa area has more game reserves than any other place in South Africa and, thanks to a decision to do away with game park fences across international boundaries, it is fast becoming the leading tourist destination in the country. Many private game resorts form part of a larger reserve; the game move around freely, allowing visitors to encounter most animal species. No two game resorts are the same – each has its own character and style.

During my travels in search of good food, hospitable people and beautiful places I have had the most extraordinary experiences, not the least of which was being invited for a flip in a microlite . . . what an experience that was! The takeoff caused strange, frightening sensations in my stomach, but once we were airborne I risked a quick downward glance – and suddenly I felt as free as an eagle gliding through the air. From up there I could see distant vistas; I watched the sun setting on one side and the dark encroaching from the other, and was overwhelmed by the beauty of Creation. And I knew that I would cherish these memories forever.

All Drifters Game Lodge guests are collected at the gate, since no ordinary car can go there. Andy Dott's company, Drifters, provides African camping safaris that are very popular, especially among foreign visitors. This is an up-market game lodge, close to the Kruger National Park. The lodge, with its thatched roof, blends into the surrounding bush and from the spacious wooden deck you can watch the animals in the riverbed below; even the open showers in the tent chalets offer breathtaking views. Kudu graze at the water hole and, a short distance away, giraffe affectionately rub their necks together. Ryan and Louise Utermark are the hosts here. Louise has had excellent training in food preparation and likes to surprise her guests by creating new dishes. Guests expect the usual braai food and are absolutely dumbfounded by the delicious creations that appear on the table.

Stuffed chicken breasts in phyllo pastry parcels

CHICKEN

6 chicken breasts, skinned and boned

1 medium-sized onion, chopped

oil

180 g (¾ container) cream cheese or creamed
  cottage cheese

6 sun-dried tomatoes, finely chopped

125 ml (½ c) chopped fresh basil

6 sheets phyllo pastry

125 g butter, melted

TOMATO COULIS

2 medium-sized onions, chopped

oil

6 sun-dried tomatoes

15 ml (1 T) sugar

1 tin (400 g) whole, peeled tomatoes

60 ml (¼ c) tomato paste

60 ml (¼ c) vegetable stock

salt and freshly ground black pepper

VEGETABLES

30 ml (2 T) butter

5 ml (1 t) lemon juice

5 ml (1 t) finely grated lemon rind

1 container sugar snap peas, thinly sliced

4 large carrots, sliced into julienne strips

Place each chicken breast between two sheets of plastic wrap and flatten slightly with a meat mallet. Sauté the onion in a little hot oil until golden brown and tender. Allow to cool. When cooled, mix with the cream cheese, sun-dried tomatoes and basil. Spread the mixture over the flattened chicken breasts and roll up tightly, like a Swiss roll. Brush a sheet of phyllo pastry with melted butter. Place another sheet of pastry on top and cut in half. Repeat with the other pastry sheets. Place a chicken roll on each piece of pastry and fold in the sides of the pastry. Wrap each chicken roll in the pastry to form a parcel. Chill the parcels until needed.

To make the coulis, stir-fry the onions in oil until golden brown. Add the sun-dried tomatoes and stir-fry for another 2 minutes. Add the sugar and heat until caramelised. Add the whole tomatoes, tomato paste and stock, and bring to the boil. Simmer for 30 minutes. Process the sauce in a food processor until smooth and season well with salt and freshly ground black pepper.

Preheat the oven to 200 °C (400 °F) and bake the chicken parcels until golden brown and done (about 20 minutes). Meanwhile, heat the butter, lemon juice and rind, and fry the vegetable strips until just done, but still crisp. Spoon the vegetables into the centre of a platter. Drizzle the hot pan juices around the vegetables. Flatten the vegetables slightly with the back of a spoon. Slice the chicken parcels in half diagonally and arrange on top of the vegetables. Drizzle the coulis around the edges. Garnish with fresh basil.

Serves 3-4.

Ostrich carpaccio with avocado and pawpaw tower

CARPACCIO

500 g ostrich fillet

60 ml (¼ c) prepared mustard

freshly ground black pepper to taste

60 ml (¼ c) olive oil

60 ml (¼ c) balsamic vinegar

60 ml (¼ c) chopped fresh mixed herbs

TOWER

1 ripe avocado

125 ml (½ c) lettuce leaves, broken
   into bite-sized pieces

juice of 1 lemon

½ ripe medium-sized pawpaw

30 ml (2 T) cider vinegar

30 ml (2 T) white sugar

PEPPADEW DRESSING

60 ml (¼ c) olive oil

60 ml (¼ c) apple vinegar

125 ml (½ c) whole peppadews

5 ml (1 t) white sugar

5 ml (1 t) prepared mustard

MAYONNAISE

60 ml (¼ c) mayonnnaise

60 ml (¼ c) cream

125 ml (½ c) chopped fresh mixed herbs

DEEP-FRIED LEEKS

2 leeks, thoroughly washed

250 ml (1 c) oil

Coat the fillet with the mustard and season with freshly ground black pepper. Sprinkle half the olive oil and vinegar over the fillet. Wrap in plastic wrap and place in the freezer until frozen.

Cube the avocado and mix lightly with the lettuce. Season well with lemon juice and black pepper. Cube the pawpaw and season generously with cider vinegar, sugar and black pepper. (Prepare the avocado and pawpaw just before serving to prevent discolouration.)

Place all the ingredients for the peppadew dressing in a food processor and process until smooth. Season to taste and set aside.

Blend the mayonnaise, cream and freshly chopped herbs and set aside.

Slice the leeks into julienne strips. Heat the oil in a saucepan until very hot and deep-fry the leek strips until golden brown and crisp. Drain on paper towelling and keep warm.

To serve: Remove the fillet from the freezer about 5 minutes before serving. Using an electric knife, slice the fillet into paper-thin slices. Arrange in a circle around the edge of a platter. Moisten with the rest of the olive oil and vinegar, and sprinkle with the chopped herbs. Spoon a little of the avocado mixture in the centre of the platter and top with a little of the pawpaw mixture. Drizzle with the mayonnaise and peppadew dressing and finish with the deep-fried leeks.

Serves 4.

Deep-fried Camembert in couscous

CAMEMBERT

125 ml (½ c) vegetable stock

125 ml (½ c) couscous

1 whole Camembert cheese

2 extra-large eggs, whisked

125 ml (½ c) cake flour

250 ml (1 c) oil

SALAD

1 punnet (250 g) strawberries, hulled

1 bunch fresh coriander leaves

½ English cucumber

15 ml (1 T) honey

30 ml (2 T) balsamic vinegar

freshly ground black pepper

CHILLI SAUCE

½ punnet (125 g) strawberries, hulled

3 ml (generous ½ t) chopped red chillies

30 ml (2 T) orange juice

10 ml (2 t) strawberry jam

Bring the vegetable stock to the boil and sprinkle the couscous on top. Remove from the heat and allow to stand so the couscous can absorb the liquid and swell up. Cut the Camembert into 8 wedges and dip in the whisked eggs, then in the cake flour, and again in the egg. Coat with the couscous, ensuring the wedges are evenly covered. Arrange the cheese wedges on a plate and chill until needed.

Quarter the strawberries and coarsely chop the coriander leaves, reserving a few whole leaves for garnishing. Slice the cucumber into strips using a potato peeler and mix with the strawberries, coriander leaves, honey and vinegar in a small bowl. Season well with black pepper.

Process all the ingredients for the chilli sauce in a food processor until smooth.

To serve: Arrange the salad in the centre of a serving platter. Remove the Camembert wedges from the fridge. Heat the oil in a small saucepan until very hot and fry the Camembert wedges until golden brown. Arrange the Camembert wedges on top of the salad, garnish with coriander leaves and serve with the sweet chilli sauce.

Serves 3-4.

Apple tarte Tatin with caramel sauce

TARTE TATIN

6 small Granny Smith apples, peeled
  and cored

lemon juice

250 ml (1 c) white sugar

60 ml (¼ c) water

pinch ground cinnamon

250 g (1 packet) frozen puff pastry, thawed

SAUCE

250 ml (1 c) sugar

60 ml (¼ c) water

To make the tarte Tatin: Preheat the oven to 190 °C (375 °F) and grease 5-6 9-cm ovenproof ramekins with butter or margarine or spray with nonstick spray.

Slice the apples into rings and place in water to which lemon juice has been added, to prevent discolouration. Meanwhile, slowly heat the sugar and water until the sugar has dissolved. Bring to the boil and boil rapidly until the syrup turns a light caramel colour. Remove from the heat immediately to prevent the caramel becoming too dark and bitter. Quickly pour the hot caramel into the ramekins and set aside to harden. Pat the apple rings dry and arrange on top of the caramel, one by one. Sprinkle each apple ring with ground cinnamon and try to fit the slices of one apple in each ramekin (the slices shrink during the baking process). Bake for 25-30 minutes or until the caramel bubbles through the apple rings. Allow to cool and chill for later use or until just before serving.

Cut out pastry circles the same diameter as the ramekins. Press a pastry circle on top of each ramekin, pressing the edges of the pastry slightly over the edge of the ramekin. Chill while preparing the caramel sauce.

To make the caramel sauce: Slowly heat the sugar and 60 ml (¼ c) water until the sugar has dissolved. Bring to a rapid boil and cook until the syrup turns a caramel brown. Add the extra 60 ml (¼ c) water, taking care, as it will spatter. Continue stirring until the caramel has melted and a rich sauce forms.

Bake the tarte Tatins for about 15 minutes until the pastry is golden brown and nicely risen. Remove from the oven and carefully turn out the tarts on individual serving plates so the apples rest on the pastry base. Serve with the caramel sauce and a scoop of vanilla ice cream.

Makes 6 tarte Tatins.

By early evening, the bush is already casting long shadows over Matumi Game Lodge, on the far side of Hoedspruit, and the setting sun colours the sky a pinkish orange. In the reception area impala graze on the lawns and the tamest of the herd approach to make our acquaintance. Elsie and Theo Rosslee moved here in the early eighties. Everyone in the area will tell you that Elsie is good at preparing meat; although she's had no formal training she makes light work of catering for four hundred people at a time out here in the bush. The Lodge is part of the Caraville Group, but it's their à la carte restaurant, in particular, that is popular. When a large number of guests are expected, they like to provide a buffet.

Matumi venison fillet

You can prepare beef fillet in the same way, says Elsie Rosslee of Matumi.

4 portions venison fillet (250 g each)

fresh lemon juice

SAUCE

250 g (1 packet) streaky bacon

½ medium-sized onion, finely chopped

1 clove garlic, crushed

250 g (1 punnet) brown mushrooms, sliced

500 ml (2 c) fresh cream

5 ml (1 t) beef stock powder

30 ml (2 T) cornflour

50 ml water

3 ml (generous ½ t) soy sauce

1 ml (¼ t) paprika

salt and freshly ground black pepper to taste

4 thin slices Cheddar cheese

Marinate the venison fillet in a little lemon juice while making the sauce. Chop the bacon and fry in a pan along with the onion, garlic and sliced mushrooms. Add the cream and heat slowly while stirring continuously. Mix the beef stock powder and cornflour with the water to form a smooth paste. Stir into the cream and bring to the boil once more, stirring continuously. Add the soy sauce, paprika, salt and pepper, and simmer slowly until the sauce is done and slightly thickened.

Braai the fillet over hot coals or on a gas braai until done to your taste. Just before removing the meat from the grid, top with a slice of Cheddar cheese, heating until the cheese has melted slightly. Serve the fillet with the sauce, a baked potato or chips, and crisp vegetables.

Serves 4.

Matumi venison stew

Pieces of oxtail add extra flavour to this dish. At Matumi they make the stew in large pots.

1 kg venison shank, cut into pieces

salt and freshly ground black pepper

oil

2 large onions, coarsely chopped

3 cloves garlic, crushed

1 oxtail, cut into pieces

pinch ground cloves

250 ml (1 c) beef stock, slightly heated

125 ml (½ c) red wine

60 ml (¼ c) fruit chutney

7 ml (1½ t) mixed dried herbs

250 ml (1 c) tomato purée

500 g baby onions

250 g (1 packet) button mushrooms

250 g baby carrots

Season the venison with salt and black pepper and brown in heated oil. Remove from the pan and set aside. Fry the onions and garlic in the pan fat until soft and fragrant. Also remove from the pan and set aside. Brown the oxtail pieces, reduce the heat and add the cloves and beef stock. Simmer until the meat is nearly tender. Add the venison, red wine and remaining ingredients, except the tomato purée and vegetables. Cover and simmer until the meat is tender. Add the tomato purée and vegetables (including the fried onions and garlic) and simmer, uncovered, until the sauce thickens and the vegetables are just done.

Serve with pearl wheat.

Serves 8-10.

The idea of starting a lodge in the bush and providing facilities for playing a round of golf at the same time, occurred to them about ten years ago during a visit to Sun City's Million Dollar Golf Tournament, says Margaret Murphy of Masorini Lodge. The unique Hans Merensky Country Club, coupled with Phalaborwa's reputation for being a town with two summers, clinched their decision to buy a small bushveld farm just north of the town.

When we were there, everything was still brand-new, and Margaret prepared our meals in her newly-equipped kitchen near the lapa. She's an ardent collector of cookery books and welcomes the opportunity to try out all her favourite recipes.

Margaret likes to experiment and she goes through phases of trying different cuisines, but in the end it's the availability of ingredients that determines her choice of menu. The food is fresh and original, incorporating new ideas for old stand-bys.

Spinach cheesecake

Served with a flavoursome tomato sauce, this spinach cheesecake is an absolute winner at Masorini.

CRUST

70 ml (4 T + 2 t) butter, melted

250 ml (1 c) Bacon Kips savoury
   biscuits, crushed

FILLING

2 bunches spinach, cleaned,
   shredded and steamed

3 rashers bacon, coarsely chopped

1 medium-sized onion, finely chopped

250 g (1 container) cream cheese
   or creamed cottage cheese

350 ml sour cream

4 extra-large eggs, whisked

125 g (2 rounds) feta cheese, crumbled

Parmesan cheese, grated

Preheat the oven to 150 °C (300 °F) and grease a 20-cm loose-bottomed cake tin with butter or margarine or spray with nonstick spray. Mix the butter and biscuit crumbs and press into the base – and partway up the sides – of the prepared cake tin. Set aside.

Drain the steamed spinach and squeeze out any excess liquid. Fry the bacon until half done, add the onion and fry until soft and fragrant. Beat the cream cheese or creamed cottage cheese, sour cream and eggs together. Add the bacon and onion mixture, spinach and feta cheese, and mix. Turn the mixture into the prepared crust and bake for 1¼ hours until firm and golden brown. Sprinkle with a little Parmesan cheese and leave for about 30 minutes until firmer. Serve lukewarm or at room temperature with a flavoursome tomato sauce (below).

Makes 1 large spinach cheesecake.

Flavoursome tomato sauce

15 ml (1 T) oil

2 large onions, finely chopped

3 cloves garlic, crushed

125 ml (½ c) tomato purée

125 ml (½ c) chutney

5 ml (1 t) prepared mustard

10 ml (2 t) Worcester sauce

60 ml (¼ c) tomato sauce

80 ml (⅓ c) sweet sherry

80 ml (⅓ c) water

5 ml (1 t) vinegar

Heat the oil and sauté the onions and garlic until soft and fragrant. Add the remaining ingredients and bring to the boil. Simmer for about 10-15 minutes until flavoursome. Serve hot or at room temperature.

Makes about 250 ml (1 c) tomato sauce.

Vegetable quiche

Margaret Murphy of Masorini Game Lodge loves spinach and often uses it in her dishes. She adapts this quiche according to what's available.

CRUST

250 ml (1 c) cake flour

2 ml (½ t) salt

3 ml (generous ½ t) baking powder

70 ml (4 T + 2 t) butter

125 ml (½ c) finely grated Cheddar cheese

1 extra-large egg yolk

45 ml (3 T) ice-cold water

FILLING

30 ml (2 T) butter

1 bunch chives, chopped

1 large red sweet pepper, coarsely chopped

250 g mushrooms, sliced

180 ml (¾ c) Kabanossi or Russian sausages,
  sliced into rings

500 g spinach, shredded and steamed
  until cooked

salt and freshly ground black pepper to taste

EGG MIXTURE

2 extra-large eggs

250 ml (1 c) sour cream

250 ml (1 c) grated Cheddar cheese

Combine the cake flour, salt and baking powder. Rub in the butter with your fingertips until the mixture resembles coarse breadcrumbs. Add the grated Cheddar cheese, egg yolk and half the water, and mix to form a pastry. Add the rest of the water if necessary. Shape the pastry into a ball, cover with plastic wrap and chill for about 30 minutes.

Meanwhile, preheat the oven to 200 °C (400 °F) and grease a 27-cm loose-bottomed quiche or cake tin with butter or margarine or spray with nonstick spray. Heat the 30 ml butter and sauté the chives, sweet pepper and mushrooms until soft and fragrant. Add the sausages and spinach. Season with salt and freshly ground black pepper and set aside.

Remove the pastry from the fridge and roll it out on a lightly floured surface. Line the prepared tin with the pastry and prick the base with a fork. Line with baking paper and sprinkle dried beans or rice over the base. Bake for about 10 minutes or until the sides of the pastry begin to brown. Remove from the oven and remove the baking paper and beans.

Spoon the filling into a colander or sieve and press with a wooden spoon to remove any excess liquid. Beat the eggs and sour cream together and season with salt and black pepper. Turn the filling into a mixing bowl, add the egg mixture and mix. Turn into the prepared pie crust. Sprinkle with grated Cheddar cheese and bake for 10 minutes at 200 °C (400 °F). Reduce the temperature to 180 °C (350 °F) and bake for another 40-50 minutes until firm and golden brown.

Makes 1 large quiche.

Layered dip

This dip is excellent served with tortilla chips, says Margaret Murphy of Masorini Game Lodge.

1 tin (410 g) chopped tomatoes (Mexican flavour)

2 ripe avocados

15 ml (1 T) lemon juice

salt and freshly ground black pepper to taste

250 ml (1 c) sour cream

250 ml (1 c) finely grated Cheddar cheese

125 ml (½ c) finely chopped chives

a little paprika and parsley to garnish (optional)

Spoon the chopped tomatoes into the bottom of a 28 cm x 18 cm dish. Peel the avocados and process with the lemon juice, salt and freshly ground black pepper in a food processor until smooth. Spoon on top of the tomato mixture, spreading evenly. Lightly mix the sour cream and grated cheese together and carefully spoon on top of the avocado layer. Sprinkle with chives and garnish with a little paprika and parsley.

Makes 1,1 litre dip.

Baked chicken schnitzels with vegetables

After they've been cooked the schnitzels are oven-baked on a bed of fragrant vegetables. Allow 2 chicken breasts per person.

CHICKEN SCHNITZELS

8 boned chicken breasts
lemon juice
freshly ground black pepper
a little cake flour
1 egg, whisked
dried breadcrumbs
butter

VEGETABLES

1 punnet courgettes, roughly sliced
500 g (2 punnets) button mushrooms, sliced

TOMATO SAUCE

1 tin (410 g) tomato and onion mix
1 small tin (25 g) tomato paste
1 clove garlic, crushed
salt and freshly ground black pepper
10 ml (2 t) basil
10 ml (2 t) origanum
Tabasco sauce to taste
5 ml (1 t) sugar
white pepper to taste
1 ml (¼ t) ground black pepper
cayenne pepper to taste

TOPPING

250 ml (1 c) sour cream
250 ml (1 c) grated Parmesan cheese

Preheat the oven to 200 °C (400 °F) and grease a 28-cm square oven dish with butter or margarine or spray with non-stick spray. (This facilitates cleaning.)

Place a chicken breast between 2 layers of wax paper or plastic wrap. Flatten slightly with a meat mallet. Place all the flattened chicken breasts in a glass container and sprinkle with lemon juice and freshly ground black pepper. Chill for a few hours, turning occasionally. Remove the chicken breasts from the lemon juice and pat dry with paper towelling. Roll in the flour, then in the egg and finally in the dried breadcrumbs. Fry gently in butter until golden brown and just done. Do not over-cook.

Sauté the courgettes in a little butter until done, but still firm. Add the mushrooms and sauté until just tender. Transfer the vegetables to the prepared oven dish.

To make the tomato sauce, heat all the ingredients for the sauce and simmer for 5-7 minutes. Pour over the vegetables in the dish. Arrange the chicken breasts on top. Mix the sour cream and cheese and spoon over the chicken breasts. Bake for 30-35 minutes until heated through.

Serve with rice and a green salad.

Serves 4.

Honey and yoghurt dip

300 ml thick cream
75 ml (5 T) honey
250 ml (1 c) Greek yoghurt

Whip the cream until it just begins to thicken. Add the honey and beat until thick. Slowly stir in the yoghurt and chill overnight. Serve with fruit salad and granola, or with a fruit tart or apple crumble.

Makes about 750 ml (3 c).

Baked chicken schnitzels with vegetables

Meringue roll

With its creamy almond filling, this roll makes a delectable dessert.

4 extra-large egg whites

180 ml (¾ c) castor sugar

5 ml (1 t) ground cinnamon

15 ml (1 T) white sugar

50 g (½ packet) flaked almonds

250 ml (1 c) cream

45 ml (3 T) icing sugar, sifted

2-3 drops almond essence

Preheat the oven to 180 °C (350 °F) and grease a Swiss roll tin with butter or margarine or spray with nonstick spray. Line with wax paper and grease or spray with nonstick spray once more. Dust with cornflour.

Beat the egg whites until soft peaks form. Add the castor sugar by the spoonful, beating after each addition. Beat until stiff and spread the meringue mixture evenly over the wax paper. Sprinkle with cinnamon, sugar and the flaked almonds. Bake for 10 minutes until the meringue is pale brown. Remove from the oven and loosen the edges of the meringue. Cover the meringue with a large sheet of wax paper and place an inverted wire rack on top. Carefully turn the meringue and rack over so the meringue rests on the wire rack. Remove the Swiss roll tin and wax paper lining and allow the meringue to cool.

Whip the cream, icing sugar and almond essence until stiff and spread over the meringue. Roll up lengthways. Serve with fresh berries, if preferred. The roll also freezes well. Thaw in the fridge.

Makes 1 medium-sized roll.

Hungarian nut torte

Our photographer, Neville Lockhart, couldn't get enough of this tart.

CAKE

250 ml (1 c) white sugar

90 ml (6 T) cake flour

5 ml (1 t) baking powder

5 ml (1 t) vanilla essence

4 extra-large eggs

150 g (1½ packets) pecan nuts

ICING

125 ml (½ c) smooth apricot jam

100 g dark chocolate

60 g butter

5 ml (1 t) vanilla essence

Preheat the oven to 180 °C (350 °F) and grease a 21-cm loose-bottomed cake tin with butter or margarine or spray with nonstick spray. Line with baking paper and grease or spray with nonstick spray once more.

Place all the ingredients for the cake in a food processor and process until the pecan nuts are finely chopped. Turn the batter into the prepared cake tin, spreading evenly. Bake for about 35-40 minutes or until a skewer comes out clean when inserted into the centre of the cake.

To make the icing, heat the apricot jam and spread over the cake. Allow to cool completely. Melt the chocolate and butter together, stirring until smooth. Remove from the heat and stir in the vanilla essence. Allow to cool slightly and spoon the icing over the cake.

Makes 1 single-layered cake.

Meringue roll

The boardwalk at Kuname River Lodge takes you to a heavy wooden door – and by then you know there is something special waiting for you. The lodge, with its thatched roof and warm colours, nestles against the river bank. On the riverside, the building is completely open; there are no doors or windows, only large openings leading to an enormous wooden deck. From this vantage point you can watch game in the riverbed through binoculars.

Peet and Erika Strydom bought the land, in the Gravelotte area, in February 1999. At first they intended retiring here, but somehow they ended up with this guesthouse in the bushveld. In October of that year the first guests arrived.

Mealtimes depend on how long game-viewing trips last. Since the nearest shop is 60 km away, Erika has had to learn to plan in advance and to take a cool bag along on shopping trips to town. Her food represents home cooking at its best; awaiting us are an unusual chicken roll and a selection of cakes. While we're taking photographs, I hear the bark of a bushbuck for the first time. Hawks circle overhead and exquisitely hued butterflies flutter around outside. I agree with our photographer when he says: "Here you can sit for hours doing nothing, and experience real life at the same time."

Chicken roll with orange sauce

Erika Strydom of Kuname River Lodge says boning a chicken requires a little practice, but once you've got the hang of it, it doesn't take long.

2 x 1,8 kg whole chickens
20 ml (4 t) olive oil

FILLING
125 g dried apricots
150 g chopped ham
250 ml (1 c) fresh breadcrumbs
250 ml (1 c) cooked rice, preferably a wild rice mix
125 ml (½ c) coarsely chopped pecan nuts
2 chives, chopped
2 extra-large eggs, lightly whisked
salt and freshly ground black pepper to taste

ORANGE SAUCE
500 ml (2 c) chicken stock
10 ml (2 t) Grand Marnier liqueur
10 ml (2 t) finely grated orange rind
5 ml (1 t) cornflour
10 ml (2 t) orange juice

Preheat the oven to 180 °C (350 °F). Bone the chickens: Cut through the breastbone and, using a sharp-pointed knife, cut down all along the ribcage. Remove the bones. Trim the wings by removing the tips. Cut through the thigh joints and remove the bones. Turn in the meat of the wings and thighs.

To make the filling, place the apricots in a small dish and pour over boiling water. Soak until the apricots are soft and plump. Mix the rest of the filling ingredients and spread evenly over the inside of the butterflied chickens. Arrange the apricots in a row on top of the filling. Roll up the chickens like a Swiss roll, tucking in the edges as you go along. Secure neatly with string and close any openings with cocktail sticks.

Pour the olive oil into an oven dish, place the chickens in the dish and oven-roast for about 1½ hours until the chickens are done and golden brown. Remove the chickens from the oven dish and place on a serving platter.

To make the orange sauce, add the sauce ingredients to the dish in which the chickens were cooked and simmer until the sauce thickens and is done. Serve with the chickens, yellow rice and chunky stir-fried vegetables.

Serves 10-12.

Buttermilk cake

Peet and Erika's daughter, Karien, always ensures there's a delicious baked treat at teatime. She's adapted the icing so it can be used with any of the cakes.

CAKE
375 ml (1½ c) white sugar

250 g butter

5 extra-large eggs, separated

5 ml (1 t) finely chopped dried
  naartjie peel

10 ml (2 t) bicarbonate of soda

500 ml (2 c) buttermilk

750 ml (3 c) cake flour

pinch salt

pinch nutmeg

ICING
250 ml (1 c) icing sugar

60 ml (¼ c) full-cream milk powder

125 g butter, softened

10 ml (2 t) vanilla essence

Preheat the oven to 180 °C (350 °F) and grease two deep 22-cm cake tins with butter or margarine or spray with nonstick spray.

Cream the sugar and butter together until light and creamy. Beat in the egg yolks one by one, beating well after each addition. Stir in the naartjie peel. Dissolve the bicarbonate of soda in the buttermilk. Sift the cake flour, salt and nutmeg together and fold into the butter mixture, alternating with the buttermilk.

Beat the egg whites until stiff peaks form and carefully fold in. Spoon into the prepared cake tins, spreading evenly. Bake for 45-50 minutes, or until a skewer comes out clean when inserted into the centre of the cake. Allow the cakes to cool for a while in the tins before turning out to cool completely on a wire rack.

Sift the icing sugar and milk powder together. Add to the butter little by little, beating well until light and creamy. Flavour with the vanilla essence. Decorate the cakes with the icing.

Makes 2 cakes.

Kuname's cake selection

Banana carrot cake

We couldn't resist second and third helpings of this delicious cake.

250 ml (1 c) white sugar
250 ml (1 c) oil
3 extra-large eggs
375 ml (1½ c) cake flour
10 ml (2 t) baking powder
10 ml (2 t) cinnamon
pinch salt
5 ml (1 t) bicarbonate of soda
250 ml (1 c) coarsely grated carrots
250 ml (1 c) mashed bananas
200 ml pecan nuts, coarsely chopped

Preheat the oven to 180 °C (350 °F) and grease a loose-bottomed ring cake tin with butter or margarine or spray with nonstick spray.

Beat the sugar and oil together and add the eggs one by one, beating well after each addition. Sift the cake flour, baking powder, cinnamon, salt and bicarbonate of soda together. Add to the sugar and oil mixture and fold in. Lightly mix in the carrots, banana and nuts. Turn the batter into the prepared cake tin and bake for 40-55 minutes or until a skewer comes out clean when inserted into the centre of the cake. Allow to cool in the tin before turning out onto a wire rack to cool completely. Ice with the same icing used to decorate the buttermilk cake (p. 235). To vary the icing, add 30 ml (2 T) Greek yoghurt to the icing. Sprinkle chopped nuts over the cake.

Makes 1 large cake.

Ant cake

The batter for this cake is made with chocolate vermicelli, which gives the cake a speckled look. Eat the cake the same day, as it tends to become a bit dry.

170 g butter, at room temperature
250 ml (1 c) castor sugar
4 extra-large eggs, separated
500 ml (2 c) cake flour
15 ml (1 T) baking powder
250 ml (1 c) coconut
100 g chocolate vermicelli
250 ml (1 c) milk

Preheat the oven to 180 °C (350 °F) and grease two 22-cm round cake tins with butter or margarine or spray with nonstick spray.

Cream the butter and castor sugar together until light and creamy. Add the egg yolks one by one, beating well after each addition. Sift the cake flour and baking powder together. Fold in along with the coconut and vermicelli. Beat the egg whites until stiff peaks form and fold into the batter, alternating with the milk. Turn the batter into the prepared cake tins and bake for about 55 minutes until done or a skewer comes out clean when inserted into the centre of the cake. Decorate with the same icing used for the buttermilk cake (p. 235), but add a little cocoa powder.

Makes 2 cakes.

As can be expected in the bushveld, Lourene Game Lodge is built of stone. Loutjie and Rene le Roux always wanted to make their home here, and while Loutjie was on a hunting trip near Gravelotte in 1996, the guide told him that the neighbouring property was for sale. They bought it there and then and named it Lourene, a combination of Loutjie and Rene. They bought game, put up fences and fixed up the house. Soon afterwards they decided to convert the place into a lodge. Lourene now also boasts a large restaurant.

Lourene meringue nests

People visit Lourene specially to indulge themselves in this sweet treat. Our photographer, who is known for his sweet tooth, could not get enough of it.

MERINGUE

6 egg whites

5 ml (1 t) cream of tartar

375 ml (1½ c) castor sugar

FILLING

500 ml (2 c) cream, chilled

1 tin (385 g) caramel condensed milk

1 tin (110 g) granadilla pulp

fresh strawberries, kiwi fruit or other berries
  for decoration

Preheat the oven to 100 °C (212 °F) and lightly dust a baking sheet with cornflour. Beat the egg whites until soft peaks form. Add the cream of tartar and beat in the castor sugar by the spoonful, beating well after each addition. Beat until the mixture is stiff and glossy. Spoon the meringue mixture into a piping bag and pipe meringue nests on the baking sheet. Lower the temperature and place in a cool oven at 60-80 °C (120-160 °F) overnight to dry out. Set aside to cool. Keep in an airtight container until needed.

Whip the cream until stiff, add three-quarters of the tin of condensed milk and beat well. Chill until set. Spoon a teaspoonful of the rest of the condensed milk into the bottom of each meringue nest. Fill a piping bag with the cream and caramel mixture and fill the meringue nests with it. Decorate with the granadilla pulp and fresh fruit. Serve immediately.

Makes 20-25 meringue nests.

Beef olives

At Lourene Game Lodge these beef olives are served with baked potatoes and a pumpkin pie.

6 x 200 g slices tenderised beef fillet

1 onion, finely chopped

2 carrots, scraped and finely chopped
  or grated

1 green sweet pepper, seeded and
  finely chopped

250 g (1 punnet) mushrooms, finely sliced

braai spice

salt and freshly ground black pepper
  to taste

Preheat the oven to 160 °C (325 °F).

Flatten the fillets. Mix the onion, carrots, sweet pepper and mushrooms and spoon a little of the mixture on top of each fillet. Sprinkle with braai spice, salt and pepper. Roll up and secure with cocktail sticks. Place the meat rolls in an ovenproof dish and spoon the rest of the vegetable mixture on top. Cover and bake until the meat is tender and done. Remove the cover and oven-roast until lightly browned on top.

Serves 4-6.

Beef olives

Index